Forensic Evidence Management

Forensic Evidence Management

Management
From the Crime Scene to the
Courtroom

Edited by
Ashraf Mozayani and Casie Parish Fisher

CRC Press
Taylor & Francis Group
Boca Raton London New York

CRC Press is an imprint of the
Taylor & Francis Group, an **informa** business

CRC Press
Taylor & Francis Group
6000 Broken Sound Parkway NW, Suite 300
Boca Raton, FL 33487-2742

Printed on acid-free paper

International Standard Book Number-13: 978-1-4987-7718-6 (Hardback)

Visit the Taylor & Francis Web site at
http://www.taylorandfrancis.com

and the CRC Press Web site at
http://www.crcpress.com

For the criminal investigators who work daily
to serve the victims of various crimes

Contents

Foreword

Evidence management has become a crucial component for the law enforcement community. As technology and technical applications continue to advance, the undertakings at crime scenes have become even more critical. Criminal investigators must ensure evidence is properly documented, collected, packaged and stored in a manner that maximizes the ability of laboratories to glean meaningful evidence.

This work is an international collaboration of subject-matter experts who have outlined and described the various evidentiary disciplines within the forensic science community. As the dynamics of a crime scene can vary dramatically, every step was taken to ensure all subject areas were addressed. In line with various regulating bodies, it strives to outline the proper collection and storage techniques for evidentiary items of crime scenes in categories familiar to criminal investigators such as biological, fingerprints, firearms and tool marks, etc. The authors take an additional step by also addressing digital/electronic evidence, forensic art, evidence within arson investigations and evidence obtained during sexual assault nurse examinations which to date does not exist in one comprehensive text. The chapter *Ethical Issues, Bias and Other Challenges to Forensic Evidence Management* addresses the issues regarding the responsibility of the criminal investigator and the challenges encountered during investigations.

I truly believe this book is invaluable for criminal investigators and can enhance many types of investigations. It can also be a valuable resource for managing evidence not often encountered.

Jeremiah Sullivan
Chairman, Board of Directors
Texas Division of the International Association for Identification
Senior Crime Scene Specialist (Retired)
Austin Police Department

Acknowledgements

I am a strong advocate for sharing knowledge and resources without any restriction. It might be because I see the globe as one country that bridging science and people seems natural to me. Assessing and auditing national and international forensic laboratories proved to me that one of the paramount facts is the collection of the appropriate evidence without cognitive bias. Ensuring that this step is done right is the basic step to find the truth in criminal and civil investigation cases. This book is a source of information for law enforcements and analysts who collect, present and store any evidence during forensic science investigation.

This source of readily accessible information would not have been possible without the unconditional assistance of my co-editor, Dr Casie Parish Fisher, and all of the contributing authors who accepted our invitation to share their time, expertise and knowledge. I also thank my colleagues and my students who with their research remind me that we must work for 'justice for all', and that it can only be done with evidence-based science. And last but not least, I never could have done this without the support of my husband Douglas, my daughter Nikou and my son Farrok. I hope this book assists and leads to better evidence collection and justice in the world for our grandchildren.

—**Ashraf Mozayani**

In life I find the greatest people are the ones you can learn the most from, and the work setting provides you considerable opportunity to embrace learning and grow with each passing day. I would first like to thank Dr Ashraf Mozayani for asking me to collaborate on this book with her. It has been challenging and rewarding and I have enjoyed interacting with the international cohort of authors from many different disciplines. To our collaborating authors, thank you! I have truly loved reading the chapters from each of you and I am thankful you agreed to be part of this project. Without your desire to further your disciplines, we could not continue to work and strive to continue to solve crimes and, ultimately, find closure and peace for the victims and families of victims. I thank Nichole Gokenbach and Marissa Valencia for their support and efforts throughout this project. I could not have made it without you both!

It should go without saying that I could not have had the time to engage in this work without the love and support of my loving husband Chris, my father Butch, my mother Charlotte and my brother Chase.

—**Casie Parish Fisher**

Contributors

Dr Ashraf Mozayani has been an internationally and nationally known forensic scientist for more than 20 years. She is the executive director of forensic sciences at the Texas Forensic Science Commission and a professor at Texas Southern University. Previously, she was the crime lab director and chief toxicologist for Harris County Institute of Forensic Science for more than 15 years. She is also an ISO international assessor and a senior forensic advisor of crime laboratories for the International Criminal Investigative Training Assistance Program and past president of the Southwestern Association of Toxicologists.

Dr Mozayani received a doctorate of pharmacy from the University of Tehran and a doctorate of pharmaceutical sciences and toxicology from the University of Alberta. She has authored and co-authored five books on topics such as crime laboratory management, drug-facilitated sexual assault and drug interaction. She is a senior forensic science advisor and instructor for the International Criminal Investigative Training Assistance Program, under the aegis of the criminal division of the U.S. Department of Justice. Dr Mozayani has been a senior forensic advisor to the governments of Uzbekistan and Thailand. She has been an International Criminal Investigative Training Assistance Program forensic science instructor for all aspects of laboratory management and toxicology laboratory operations in countries such as Morocco, Sri Lanka, Egypt and Turkmenistan. Dr Mozayani has testified as an expert witness in forensic toxicology and pharmacology in the states of Texas, Virginia, Maryland, Oklahoma, Florida, Kansas, California, Idaho and Montana, the Federal Court in Massachusetts and numerous military courts of the United States.

Dr Casie Parish Fisher has a BS in forensic science from Baylor University, an MSc in DNA profiling and a PhD in forensic and investigative sciences (forensic genetics) from the University of Central Lancashire in Preston, England. Her PhD research primarily focused on the ability to use direct amplification to develop DNA profiles from surfaces which have been processed with field techniques such as fingerprint powders and blood enhancement chemicals.

Dr Fisher has worked as a crime scene technician with the Austin Police Department and as a DNA analyst at the Texas Department of Public Safety Combined DNA Index System Laboratory. For the past 7 years, she has been the director of the Forensic Science Program at St Edward's University where she oversees two degree programs. She is a coeditor of the anthology *Pioneering Research in Forensic Science: Readings from the Primary Source Literature*, and coauthor with Christine R. Ramirez of the *Crime Scene Processing and Investigation Workbook* which complements the text written by Ross Gardner. Dr Fisher is involved in numerous organizations including the Texas Division of the International Association for Identification where she has served on the Board of Directors, as chair of the Student Membership Committee and standing chair of the Host Committee. She is currently the second vice president.

Dr Patrick Buzzini is an associate professor in forensic science with the Department of Forensic Science at Sam Houston State University. Dr Buzzini graduated with both a BS and MS in forensic science from the oldest forensic science academic institution in the world, the *Institut de Police Scientifique* of the School of Criminal Sciences with the University of Lausanne, in Switzerland. He obtained a doctoral degree in forensic science from the same institution in 2007. Dr Buzzini has more than 15 years of experience as an instructor, researcher and caseworker in criminalistics, with emphasis in trace evidence. He has developed numerous courses in criminalistics, trace evidence, questioned documents, and physical evidence interpretation at both undergraduate and graduate levels. He has authored and co-authored numerous publications in peer-reviewed scientific journals, with emphasis in trace evidence. He has also delivered multiple oral and poster presentations at forensic conferences nationally and internationally. Dr Buzzini has organized workshops and training sessions to practitioners in the field (i.e. forensic laboratory personnel) nationally and internationally as well as continuing education courses to the legal community (defense counselors, prosecuting attorneys, and judges). His research interests include the forensic applications of microscopical and spectroscopic methods (i.e. Raman spectroscopy) to various types of trace evidence and questioned documents as well as addressing problems of physical evidence interpretation. Dr Buzzini is also a consulting expert in criminalistics.

Laurie Charles, MSN, RN, SANE-A, SANE-P, is a clinical assistant professor at Texas A&M University in the newly formed Forensic Health Care Program. Ms Charles obtained her master's degree in health care management and leadership in 2015. She is an emergency department nurse who began her forensic nursing career in a paediatric hospital where she was a sexual assault nurse examiner and then manager of the forensic nursing program for 16 years. In her forensic nursing career, she cared for several thousand patients and oversaw the care of tens of thousands of patients. Additionally, Ms Charles was a sexual assault nurse examiner trainer for the

Texas Attorney General, providing education for registered nurses. She has extensive sexual assault patient care experience, but her primary expertise is in child physical abuse/neglect, child sexual abuse/assault and human trafficking. Her current focus in on outreach, providing education and training for health care professionals.

Dr Jasmine Drake is an assistant professor and laboratory coordinator of the forensic science learning laboratory at Texas Southern University, Houston. Dr Drake received a doctorate in chemistry from Louisiana State University and pursued post-doctoral studies at the National Institute of Standards and Technology. Dr Drake worked as a forensic chemist for the Drug Enforcement Administration, where her primary professional responsibilities included identification and analysis of controlled substance evidence. She is a member of the Criminalistics Section of the American Academy of Forensic Science and a governor-appointed member of the Texas Forensic Science Commission.

Sandra R Enslow is a 23-year forensic art veteran of the Los Angeles County Sheriff's Department. She manages a Forensic Art Unit at the Homicide Bureau. She has a bachelor's degree in illustration from California State University, Los Angeles and has trained with the LASD and FBI. Ms Enslow lectures on forensic art to law enforcement organizations and schools including the LASD Homicide Investigation School and Detective College. She is a fellow of the American Academy of Forensic Sciences and presents there on forensic art.

Anthony B Falsetti is a board-certified forensic anthropologist and professor of practice at the Arizona State University. He is currently collaborating with colleagues at Phoenix Children's Hospital using anonymized CT scans to collect 3D data for purposes of establishing new aging standards and to improve our understanding of facial growth in sub-adults as well as examining the use of geographic information system-based methods to help resolve missing persons' cases.

Catyana R Falsetti is a board-certified forensic artist with over 15 years' experience creating forensic facial reconstruction, post-mortem images, image clarifications, composites and age progressions. She has a master's degree in forensic science from the George Washington University. Ms Falsetti has worked at multiple law enforcement agencies including the Broward Sheriff's Office as a full-time forensic artist and has had training from the FBI and National Center for Missing and Exploited Children.

Jack Flanders, CLPE, CCSI, has 8 years of experience in an accredited Texas crime laboratory processing and comparing latent prints and more than 9 years of experience comparing friction ridge detail. He holds both Latent

Print and Crime Scene Investigator certifications through the International Association for Identification. Mr Flanders has served on the Latent Print and Crime Scene Advisory Boards for the crime laboratory and Board of Directors for the Texas Division of the International Association for Identification. He graduated from the National Forensic Academy and was the 2015 Session XLI recipient of the Dr Bill Bass award. Mr Flanders is an instructor for Texas A&M Engineering and Extension Service and the National Forensic Academy.

Dr Zeno Geradts has worked since 1991 at the Netherlands Forensic Institute as a forensic scientist. He has worked in the digital evidence department since 1997. He received a PhD from the University of Utrecht in 2002. His research focused on computational comparing of forensic images. He has been the chairman of the Engineering Section of the American Academy of Forensic Sciences and since 2008–2010 chairman of the Digital Evidence and and Multimedia section. He was elected by the section as a member of the Board of Directors of the American Academy of Forensic Sciences from 2010 to 2013. He was vice president of the American Academy of Forensic Sciences 2015–2016 and treasurer 2015–2016. He is chairman of the European Network of Forensic Science Institutes Forensic IT working group. He has published many papers in forensic journals and written many book chapters. He is active in casework as an expert witness and works on digital evidence projects.

Carol Henderson is the founding director of the National Clearinghouse for Science, Technology and the Law and a professor of law at Stetson University College of Law. Professor Henderson has presented more than 300 lectures and workshops worldwide on scientific evidence, courtroom testimony and professional responsibility. She has more than 90 publications including 'Sleuthing Scientific Evidence Information on the Internet', 106 J. *Crim. L & Criminology* 59 (2016). Professor Henderson has appeared in national media as a legal analyst and testified before Congress. She is a past president of the American Academy of Forensic Sciences (2008–2009) and current co-chair of the Life and Physical Sciences Division of the American Bar Association's Science and Technology Law Section. She is the deputy editor-in-chief of the *Sci Tech Lawyer*. She also serves on the American Bar Association Judicial Division Forensic Science Committee and as faculty for the National Judicial College.

Adam H Itzkowitz is a Florida-licensed attorney, practicing primarily in civil litigation, business, employment and hospitality law. He graduated cum laude from Stetson University College of Law, where he also received a certificate of concentration in Advocacy and the William F. Blews award for pro bono service. Mr Itzkowitz interned at the Sixth Judicial Circuit for the Honourable Amy M. Williams in the Family Division and the Honourable Thane Covert in the Criminal Division. He lectures at law schools on topics including the federal rules of evidence, hotel law and commercial transactions. He is the author of 'How Blood Evidence Led Toward, Away & Back to O.J.', which discusses how the O.J. Simpson trial could have been litigated differently given today's scientific and technological advancements. He is currently the law and science fellow at the National Clearinghouse for Science, Technology and the Law and an attorney at Westchase Law, P.A.

Michael Kessler spent 9 years in law enforcement and held positions as a deputy sheriff, police officer, crime scene analyst and special agent. In 2009, he left law enforcement and spent more than 5 years as a biometric/forensic subject matter expert for the U.S. Department of Defense including more than 4 years with the U.S. Special Operations Command. Mr Kessler's defence experience includes biometric/forensic research and development, training U.S. and allied special operations forces, forensic exploitation of improvised explosive devices and full spectrum exploitation activities including the first deployment of rapid DNA in support of military operations. His operational experience includes five deployments to Iraq, Afghanistan and the Horn of Africa in support of the global war on terrorism. He has been a certified crime scene analyst since 2007 and is a current member of the OSAC CSI Subcommittee, and remains active in numerous forensic organizations. Mr Kessler holds a BA in criminal justice-forensics from American Public University.

Michal Pierce was appointed as the quality director for the Harris County Institute of Forensic Sciences in 2013. In this position, she is responsible for overseeing the operations of the quality management division, as well as ensuring that all services provided by the agency are reliable and of high quality. Ms Pierce has been with the HCIFS for nine years. Originally hired in 2007 in the Forensic Genetics Laboratory, she served as the laboratory's QA/Compliance Manager from 2011 to 2013. Ms Pierce received her Bachelor of Science in Microbiology from the University of Illinois, followed by a Master of Science in Forensic Science from Sam Houston State University. She is certified by the American Board of Criminalistics in Molecular Biology and by the American Society for Quality as a certified manager of quality/organizational excellence.

Dr Michelle Sanford is certified as a member of the American Board of Forensic Entomology and is the forensic entomologist for the Harris County Institute of Forensic Sciences. She received her BS in Biology with an Entomology minor (2000) and MS in Entomology (2003) from the University of California, Riverside. After working in the laboratory for several years on mosquitoes she went on to pursue a PhD in Entomology from Texas A&M University (2010), investigating learning behavior in mosquitoes. As a doctoral student, she was selected for the Fulbright Student Program (2008) to conduct research in Thailand at Chiang Mai University. Following her PhD, she pursued post-doctoral training at the University of California, Davis in the population genetics of malaria mosquitoes. In 2013, she joined the Harris County Institute of Forensic Sciences as the first fulltime forensic entomologist employed by a medical examiner's office in the United States.

Jay M Stuart has a BS in chemistry. He has worked in the field of firearm/tool mark examination for almost a decade, working with both the SE Missouri Regional Crime Laboratory and the Albuquerque Police Department. A graduate of the BATFE's National Firearm Examiner Academy (2004–2005), Mr Stuart is currently the technical leader of the Firearm/Tool Mark Unit at the Albuquerque Police Department. A distinguished member of the Association of Firearm and Tool Mark Examiners, he is one of the few forensic scientists to be certified in all three areas offered: Firearm Evidence Examination and Identification, Tool Mark Evidence Examination and Identification and Gunshot Residue Evidence Examination and Identification. Mr Stuart is heavily involved with the Association of Firearm and Tool Mark Examiners. He has published numerous papers in the *Association of Firearm and Tool Mark Examiners Journal* and given presentations at the Association of Firearm and Tool Mark Examiners Annual Training Seminars. He is a member (or chair) of multiple association committees.

Ryan Swafford is a 2017 graduate of Stetson University College of Law. He was Professor Carol Henderson's research assistant, working on topics including forensic evidence management and ethical considerations within the scientific and legal communities. Mr Swafford assisted in the drafting and publication of articles such as 'Sleuthing Scientific Evidence Information on the Internet', published in *The Journal of Criminal Law and Criminology*, Vol. 106, No. 1, which provided various online resources available for forensic science disciplines. He clerked for Bajo, Cuva, Turkel and Cohen during his second and third years of law school. He served as Parliamentarian for the Real Property and Probate Trust Law organization at Stetson University College of Law.

Cassandra Velasquez has worked 10 years in law enforcement support. She has held positions as a police dispatcher, 911 operator, driver's license administrative assistant, evidence technician, crime lab specialist and investigative specialist including crime scene response and evidence management. Mrs Velasquez has been a member of the Texas Association of Property and Evidence Technicians since 2008 and holds an advanced certification. She became a member of the International Association for Property and Evidence in 2009 and became a certified property and evidence specialist in 2015. She has authored evidence packaging manuals, standard operating procedures and training manuals for multiple law enforcement agencies. Mrs Velasquez has a BA in ancient history and classical civilization from the University of Texas, Austin.

Dr Jason Wiersema is director of Forensic Investigations and Emergency Management at the Harris County Institute of Forensic Sciences. He is also a diplomate of the American Board of Forensic Anthropology and conducts forensic anthropological analysis for the institute. Dr Wiersema holds adjunct faculty positions at the Baylor College of Medicine and the University of Texas Health Science Center, Houston. He serves on numerous local, state and federal advisory committees and working groups. He is chair of the Disaster Victim Identification Subcommittee of the Organization of Scientific Area Committees. He has numerous peer-reviewed publications. Dr Wiersema received his PhD in physical anthropology from Texas A&M University in 2006. His professional and research interests focus on mass fatality response and preparedness, as well as trauma analysis and interpretation.

Dr Claire Williamson, BSc, MSc, has a PhD in forensic science from the University of Central Lancashire, UK specializing in analytical techniques to analyse documents and inks. She has 10 years of teaching experience at university level contributing to undergraduate and post-graduate courses and is course leader for MSc document analysis at the University of Central Lancashire. Dr Williamson is a member of the Chartered Society of Forensic Sciences and a fellow of the Higher Education Academy. She has consulted on a range of cases and works closely with document examiners in the United Kingdom.

Kenneth Wilson has been the fire marshal and chief arson investigator for the City of Azle, Texas for over 10 years. He holds a master peace officer license, master arson investigator certification and is a TCOLE and TCFP instructor as well as a certified fire investigator with the International Association of Arson Investigators and Forensic Investigator I. Mr Wilson has worked in many aspects of law enforcement for over 30 years, including patrol, gang enforcement, CID and SWAT. He has been a certified arson investigator for over 33 years, working hundreds of arson and explosive cases and has been a member of the Tarrant County Fire and Arson Task Force for more than 15 years. He currently serves as a director and CFI chairman for the Texas chapter of the International Association of Arson Investigators, Training Committee for the Tarrant County Fire and Arson Investigators Association and is a member of the Texas Science Advisory Work Group. He conducts the International Association of Arson Investigators's Expert Witness Courtroom Testimony Course throughout Texas, preparing fire and arson investigators to provide expert testimony in trial and depositions. Mr Wilson is often called upon by other agencies to assist in properly documenting and collecting evidence at major crime scenes. Kenny was recognized by ATAC – A Texas Advisory Council on Arson with the 2015 Special Service Award for arson training.

Allison Woody serves as the manager of forensic investigations and emergency management at the Harris County Institute of Forensic Sciences. She co-manages the daily medicolegal death investigations operations and is responsible for developing and delivering fatality management and disaster response plans, trainings, and exercises. Ms Woody is also responsible for regional mass fatality management education and collaboration, including coordinating the nationwide 2013 Mass Fatality Management Symposium in Houston and numerous other workshops and conferences. Ms Woody is a founding member of the Texas Mass Fatality Operations Team (TMORT) Steering Committee, a member of the Texas Medical Incident Support Team, and the Executive Secretary for the Organization of Scientific Area Committee Disaster Victim Identification Subcommittee. In 2014, Ms Woody earned her certification as a master exercise practitioner from FEMA's Emergency Management Institute.

Jorn Chi-Chung Yu is an Associate Professor in the Department of Forensic Science at Sam Houston State University. He completed his undergraduate and graduate degrees both in Forensic Science from Central Police University in Taiwan. He earned his PhD in Chemistry from Carleton University, Ottawa, Canada. Dr Yu has more than 8 years of practical forensic working experience with the Forensic Science Center in Taipei, Taiwan, and more than 10 years of teaching and research experience in the field of forensic science. Dr Yu is a Fellow with the American Academy of Forensic Sciences. He also holds a forensic certificate (Diplomat-ABC) with the American Board of Criminalistics in the certification area of comprehensive criminalistics. His research interest is in the areas of trace evidence examination and crime scene reconstruction. The ultimate goal in his research laboratory is to develop investigative intelligence by forensic analysis of physical evidence.

Dr Nathalie Zahra, BSc (Hons), MSc, PhD, has over 15 years in the field of forensic science. She specializes in molecular biology and forensic genetics. Dr Zahra is currently a lecturer in forensic biology at Anglia Ruskin University, Cambridge. Her main research interest is in the recovery of DNA from trace evidence and touch DNA, predictable genetic markers and the use of the latest technology for the analysis of DNA. Dr Zahra is also qualified in fingerprint comparison and has acted as an independent fingerprint expert to the Court of Justice, Malta.

Crime Scene Dynamics

1

MICHAEL KESSLER AND
CASIE PARISH FISHER

Contents

Overview

Crime scene investigation is the first step of the forensic investigation process and the handling of a crime scene establishes the quality and quantity of information available for the investigation and ultimately the information available as evidence in court. The proper identification, documentation, collection and preservation of physical evidence at a crime scene are the critical first steps in ensuring the integrity and admissibility of the physical evidence. No other stage in the investigative process has such potential to impact every other stage. Any failures during this vital stage in the forensic investigative process can taint the evidence and render any further forensic analysis inadmissible.

The integrity and chain of custody of each item of evidence are initially established at its point of collection from a location associated with a crime. A crime scene may be the location where the primary offense occurred or a secondary location such as a vehicle, residence or any other object that may produce physical evidence of value to the investigation. Therefore, the responsibility of ensuring the integrity and admissibility of physical evidence is not incumbent upon only law enforcement personnel specifically tasked

1

with crime scene investigation duties, but all personnel who may come into contact with, handle or collect physical evidence.

Additionally, all items of physical evidence related to a crime may not be initially identifiable as such. Abandoned or found property may materialize into evidence critical to an investigation and should be documented, collected, packaged and stored in a manner that maintains the integrity and chain of custody of the item. While the resources and time applied to the abandoned or found property scenes will undoubtedly differ from those applied to a recognized crime scene, the general principles of sound evidence management will not change. This universal application of property and evidence collection standards to a greater or lesser extent at all scenes provides a solid foundation for further forensic analysis and judicial proceedings.

Scene Security

Principal to the successful management of evidence at the crime scene is scene security. Responding law enforcement officers – after ensuring no immediate threats remain and rendering emergency care – must secure persons on the scene and the scene itself. After an initial assessment of the scene, establishing a scene perimeter and controlling access to the scene are necessary to the safeguarding of scene integrity, preservation of evidence and minimizing contamination. Once boundaries have been established and the scene is clear of unauthorized persons, the entry and exit of all persons must be controlled and documented to maintain the integrity of the scene. This entry/exit log documentation should include approximate arrival time for all first responders and any other personnel who arrived prior to the establishment of a log. Dispatch logs may be used to supplement arrival times for first responders. The entry/exit log should be maintained until the release of the scene.

Scene Integrity

The condition of the scene as found by the first responding officers should be maintained and documented. Excepting disruptions caused by the rendering of medical care or safety concerns, neither the scene nor the involved parties (suspect, victim) should be altered. As far as possible, physical evidence should be preserved in the original state in which it was found. Once a scene has been fully secured, all items inside the scene should also be considered secured. Any items or weapons within the scene, including firearms, should not be moved unless necessary for the safety and well-being of persons on scene. Any disruptions to the scene (or any items within it) from the condition found by initial responding officers must be documented in their report.

Any manipulation of the scene including for medical or safety reasons must be documented. Undocumented changes to the scene and items within it degrade the evidence, bring the investigating agency's credibility into question and are likely to negatively affect forensic analysis and lead to the inadmissibility of the physical evidence.

For example, should the first officer to arrive on scene to a suicide disturb the scene (whether out of curiosity, negligence or for safety reasons) by moving a revolver located adjacent to the decedent's hand by picking up the firearm; opening, inadvertently rotating and then closing the cylinder; and then placing the revolver several feet away from the decedent – all without documenting those actions – would undoubtedly cause errors in further scene and forensic analysis. Moving the revolver and altering the cylinder position would alter the scene and the evidence causing investigators to pursue the investigation as a homicide as the altered scene and evidence point in that direction. By documenting his actions and reasoning, the responding officer can easily account for the scene and physical evidence being found by forensic investigators in a condition that supports a homicide hypothesis despite the incident being a suicide.

To ensure the safety of personnel and the integrity of the scene, access should be limited to personnel directly involved with processing of the scene. Contamination control can be exercised through the utilization of established entry and exit routes; collection of elimination samples from responders and investigators; use of personal protective equipment (PPE); cleaning and sanitizing tools, equipment and PPE between contact with samples and between scenes; and utilizing single-use or disposable equipment when collecting samples.

Scene Walk-Through and Initial Documentation

After assessing the scene to determine the type and level of investigation to be conducted and developing a plan for the coordinated identification, documentation and collection of physical evidence; the preliminary documentation should be prepared. Preliminary documentation includes notes and rough scene sketches of the location as they were found by investigators during an initial walk-through. This initial documentation may include the investigator's own relevant observations of the condition of the crime scene and items within it as well as information from first responders that relates to changes made to the crime scene due to medical intervention or for safety reasons during the time period between the initial response and the arrival of the investigator. While the first responders may relay such information to investigators, the investigators should request that the first responders include the information in their own reports.

The initial walk-through also serves as the first opportunity for investigators to identify valuable and fragile physical evidence. At this point, consideration should be given to whether additional resources are needed to fully process the scene, the order in which evidentiary items are collected and the order of scene processing.

Evidence Recognition and Observation

Forensic investigation depends on forensic and investigative professionals' ability to recognize physical evidence at a scene as having potential investigative or evidentiary value. This consequently relies on the training and experience of the personnel involved. While the formation of alternate hypotheses should not be constrained, information from first responders, victims and witnesses may be used to form an initial hypothesis as to what physical evidence may be relevant. The investigator should look for anything that may be out of place, as well as focusing on items that are dictated by the initial hypothesis. The recognition, documentation, collection and preservation of suitable and sufficient physical evidence play a vital role in subsequent analytical and judicial processes.

Once physical evidence is determined to be of potential evidentiary value, the preservation of that evidence becomes of paramount importance. Generally, the collection of items of evidentiary value follows thorough documentation of the scene and the items in situ; however, the presence of certain transient types of evidence, exigent environmental conditions or certain scene considerations may require collection of the items or samples before complete documentation occurs. Such transient sample types include trace evidence (hairs/fibres) in outdoor or unenclosed scenes. Environmental conditions such as rain or snow pose a substantial threat to exposed biological samples while winds can threaten numerous types of evidence in outdoor scenes. Scene considerations such as civil unrest, proximity to waterways or storm sewers may threaten the loss or destruction of physical evidence. In any circumstance, the necessity to exigently collect evidentiary items – along with any damage done to the item prior to collection – should be thoroughly documented in the investigator's report.

Scene Documentation

Recording the condition, position and location of physical evidence prior to collection provides critical information and context to the investigation. A well-documented scene ensures the integrity of the investigation and provides a permanent record for later evaluation. Failure to accurately and completely document the crime scene may negatively impact follow-on forensic analysis including crime scene reconstruction and judicial proceedings. In general, the position of bodies and of significant forensic material should be recorded prior to removal, collection or alteration.

Documentation includes notes, diagrams/sketches/3D scanning/metrology, photography, videography, etc. The initial assessment of the scene will determine the type(s) of documentation necessary for the scene investigation.

Notes

Notes should be taken continuously throughout the scene investigation. Included in the documentation should be observations of the scene as it appears and items deemed to be of potential evidentiary value. In addition to contextual data about the scene (date, location, time) transient evidence (odours, sounds) and conditions (weather, temperature) should also be noted. Just as any processing done on scene should be documented, so should any situations which require deviation from standard procedures. Audio recording may also be used to record observations and actions at a scene. The recording should include an equivalent level of detail to that of written notes.

Diagrams/Sketches/3D Scanning

A diagram presents the circumstances and positions in which evidentiary items were located in a scene. Diagrams of the crime scene, together with other relevant documentation, should enable all items of potential evidentiary value to be located at the scene and the relation of such evidence items to other objects and evidence items. Diagraming is used to specifically describe the location of items of potential evidentiary value in situ prior to collection, the location of items of potential evidentiary value relative to other objects present and other potential evidentiary items, and the physical scene. Diagrams are generally presented to scale to accurately convey the size, shape and position of significant items and other features of a crime scene. A rough sketch or multiple rough sketches may be used to note the location of objects and evidence items within the scene, serve to supplement written or verbal notes and document measurements for use in creating the finished diagram. To ensure the precision of all measurements, the accuracy of all measuring devices should be ensured by comparison to a measure of certified accuracy, such as a National Institute of Standards and Technology (NIST) traceable ruler. If objects must be moved to allow measurements to be taken, they should be photographed and their location should be marked prior to movement.

Accurate scale diagrams can also be produced using specialized imaging equipment such as laser scanning systems. The employment of these systems should be reserved to investigators trained in their use and their measurement accuracy should also be verified.

Photography

Crime scene photography (digital imaging) is a significant part of the documentation of a crime scene utilized to illustrate the scene, its contents and the condition of both. Additionally, photographic documentation of the persons involved in the incident under investigation should be undertaken to record their appearance and condition. Photographs are generally taken based on the perspective of the camera to the target and include overall, mid-range and close-up images. The scene should be fully photographed prior to alteration – this includes the placing of evidence marking placards or tents. Ideally, close-up images will be taken without and with a scale. Specialized photographic techniques should be applied to document impression evidence (footwear, tire tread, friction ridge skin, toolmarks, etc.).

Photographs are potential evidence, may become court exhibits and must remain traceable at all times. Note-taking should occur throughout the photographic documentation of the scene including the order and location of images as well as any changes made to the scene to facilitate photography. Digital images should never be deleted from the camera or digital media memory. Digital images should be stored appropriately to ensure long-term integrity. Image processing or enhancement of an original image should only be performed on working copies once original images have been safeguarded.

Videography

Just like photography, videography serves to further document the scene, its contents and the condition of both. Videography serves to supplement, but not replace, traditional photography. Videography should capture the entire scene, its contents and include the items of potential evidentiary value using overall, mid-range and close-up video. Just as photography should occur prior to alteration, including placing of evidence markers, so should videography. As each videography session should occur in an uninterrupted, systematic manner, planning of the videography route is advisable.

Accordingly, videotape or digital video files should not be deleted or destroyed. Any image enhancement or processing should also be conducted on working copies ensuring that the originals are secured.

Collection

The different types of physical evidence encountered require different skill sets to ensure that collection of evidentiary items is appropriate for the circumstances.

General guidelines for the investigator are to:

- Collect items or samples from items that are sufficient for further forensic examination. The type of examinations the item will be subjected to should be taken into consideration.
- Collect appropriate control and known samples.
- Avoid collecting material that is not relevant to the investigation or does not provide relevant information.
- Minimize potential contamination or cross-contamination of the items collected. Care should be taken to avoid cross-contamination between involved persons, victims, evidence items, equipment, the collector and scenes. Victim and suspect samples should be collected and packaged separately. Tools utilized in collection or sampling should be disposable or suitably cleaned and sanitized between samples. All collection equipment and packaging should be sterile and DNA free. Appropriate PPE should be worn.
- Consider the potential forensic impact of sampling from items versus collection of the entire item. In some instances the sample and the item on which it is situated may be collected. In other instances the entire item may itself be collected. In all instances the collection should fit the purpose.
- Place collected items in appropriate packaging.

While the overall approach to collection should be systematic, objective, thorough, planned and documented, the following chapters detail the specific considerations necessary for the proper collection, preservation and packaging of each type of physical evidence.

Bibliography

Baxter, E., Jr. (2015). *Complete Crime Scene Investigation Handbook*. Boca Raton, FL: CRC Press.

Bureau of Justice Assistance, National Institute for Standards and Technology, and National Institute of Justice. (2013). *Crime Scene Investigation: A Guide for Law Enforcement*. Largo, FL: National Forensic Science Technology Center.

Gardner, R. M. (2005). *Practical Crime Scene Processing and Investigation*. Boca Raton, FL: CRC Press.

James, S. H., and Nordby, J. J. (Eds.). (2005). *Forensic Science: An Introduction to Scientific and Investigative Techniques*. Boca Raton, FL: CRC Press.

National Institute of Justice. (2000). *A Guide for Explosion and Bombing Scene Investigation.* (NCJ Number 181869). Rockville, MD: National Criminal Justice Reference Service.

National Institute of Justice. (2000). *Fire and Arson Scene Evidence: A Guide for Public Safety Personnel.* (NCJ Number 181584). Rockville, MD: National Criminal Justice Reference Service.

National Institute of Justice. (2008). *Electronic Crime Scene Investigation: A Guide for First Responders* (2nd ed.). (NCJ Number 219941). Rockville, MD: National Criminal Justice Reference Service.

National Institute of Justice. (2011). *Death Investigation: A Guide for the Scene Investigator.* (NCJ Number 234457). Rockville, MD: National Criminal Justice Reference Service.

Robinson, E. M. (2010). *Crime Scene Photography* (2nd ed.). Burlington, MA: Academic Press.

Evidence Tracking and Secure Storage

2

CASSANDRA VELASQUEZ

Contents

Collection of evidence at a crime scene is the beginning step in the life cycle of an evidentiary item. The goal of this chapter is to address the importance of accurate tracking for evidentiary items and the need for a secure storage location. Accurate tracking and a secure storage location are essential to maintaining the integrity of evidentiary items collected during an investigation. This will be of the utmost importance so that the item can be presented during a trial.

A solid foundation for integrity begins with a written policy that clearly states the agency's overview of expectation which complies with state and federal law. Written policy is essential to create consistent practices and ensure accuracy of an agency's records. Agencies working with outdated policies increase their risk for discrepancy. Once an established policy is in place, it is imperative the administration and supervisors enforce its practice. A basic agency policy should cover the following topics:

- Statement of purpose
- Utilization and deployment
- Goals, objectives and performance measures
- Personnel duties, authority and responsibility
- Training and development
- Security
- Inspections – Audits, inventories, refrigeration standards and high-security items
- Records management and special reporting
- Release guidelines
- Disposal guidelines

To further ensure consistency within an agency, a standard operating procedure manual can be developed to provide staff with detailed documentation on the specific steps required for evidence collection, storage, transfers, analysis and disposition. These documents may require frequent updating to ensure best practices are continually met. The following areas are general topics to be addressed:

- Staff responsibilities
- Packaging guideline
- Intake procedure and storage requirements
- Report writing/record keeping
- Laboratory submissions
- Laboratory returns
- Temporary releases
  - Detective/officers
  - Court personnel
  - Crime scene technicians
- Release to owner procedure
- Evidence disposal
  - Firearms
  - Drugs
  - Currency
  - Auction/charitable items
  - Landfill items

The chronological tracking of possession and storage of an item from the time of collection to the item's final disposition is called the chain of custody. Once an item is in the custody of a law enforcement agency, the chain begins and continues to be tracked as the item travels from officer to storage, from storage to lab for analysis, from lab to court, from court back to originating agencies and ends with the item's final disposal.

Agencies track this information in order to prove an item has not been tampered with and will be available for the prosecution. When an item is submitted for analysis, the laboratory will continue tracking the item while in their possession. This creates a solid information trail for every item in the agency's care. This retrievable information can then be utilized by both the prosecuting and defence attorneys to prove the integrity of the evidence being presented in court is intact and admissible.

Current technology provides various options for tracking evidence ranging from high-tech software to traditional hardcopy evidence receipts. If an agency has the available funding, using a computerized system specifically designed for evidence management can greatly increase the efficiency of evidence handling. With the improvements and availability of cloud-based servers and WiFi, many software systems can be utilized while at a crime scene or from a patrol vehicle. This new technology has allowed many agencies to modernize their practices and eliminate hardcopy records. If funding is not available, detailed tracking can be accomplished using hardcopy evidence receipts (Figure 2.1).

For any item coming into an agency's possession the following information needs to be captured at the time of collection:

- Agency case number
- Collected by
- Date/time collected
- Item numbers – A unique identifier for each item evidence collection list
- Item description
- Collection location

Evidence receipt

Agency name case no.

| Custodian use only |
| Storage location |

Offense:
Collection location:
Collected by: Date/time:

Item #	Item description

Chain of custody

Item #	Received by:	Transfer purpose	Date:	Item #	Received by:	Transfer purpose	Date:

Figure 2.1 Example of a hardcopy evidence receipt.

Evidence collection sheet				
Agency name	Agency case number#:			Collection date:_____
Item number:	Item description:	Collection location:	Collection time:	Collected by:

Figure 2.2 Evidence collection sheet.

At a minimum, this information needs to be notated on the evidence collection list (Figure 2.2) and the outer packaging of the item (Figure 2.3). This can be accomplished by a handwritten notation on the outer packaging or with a computerized label with barcode or QR code.

Following collection and proper packaging, each change in possession needs to be documented prior to submission for secure storage. The change in possession will be documented with a chain-of-custody log (hardcopy or electronic). Ensure the chain-of-custody information is retrievable and there is only one active chain-of-custody record. It is necessary to continue documenting an item's movement within the storage location and releases (to detectives, laboratory testing, and court) and final disposal. A signature (electronic or hand-written) should be captured each time an item is released to an individual.

Proper Packaging and Proper Seals

Regardless of which tracking method your agency employs, proper packaging must be standard practice in order to ensure long-term integrity of the evidence.

Figure 2.3 Label on brown paper bag.

Some standard packaging materials for common items are listed below:

- Adhesive tape (tamper-proof tape)
- Paper bags (various sizes)
- Cardboard boxes (gun boxes, knife boxes, etc.)
- Paper envelopes (various sizes: 6 × 9 in., 9 × 12 in. and 11 × 15 in.)
- Syringe and safety tubes
- Metal cans (various sizes)
- Plastic buckets (various sizes)
- Integrity plastic bags (currency packaging)
- Kraft paper (recommend using white paper only)
- Warning labels (biohazard, fragile, etc.)

A large number of evidence items will fit inside an envelope; this type of outer packaging allows for easy storage and organization. Organic items such as plant material or item(s) with potential DNA evidence should be packaged in breathable material like paper bags or cardboard boxes. Wet or bloody items should be dried prior to packaging and then secured in a breathable container like a paper bag or cardboard box. Knives and other sharp objects should be stored in cardboard knife boxes or large plastic safety tubes. When the sharp edge is too large (i.e. swords, machetes, sickles or other tools) cardboard or puncture-resistant material should be secured around the blade to reduce the risk of injury. Liquids should be packaged in spill-proof containers such as metal cans or buckets. Kraft paper can be used for wrapping large items and covering drying areas to catch and preserve debris.

Once the outer packaging is labelled with all applicable case information, a proper seal must be applied to the container. Adhesive or tamper-proof tape should be placed across any opening of the outer package. The evidence collector will then write their initials, employee number/badge number (if applicable) and the date the container was sealed across the tape ensuring it is half on the outer packaging and half on the tape (Figure 2.4). This sealing technique allows for easy identification of tampering.

Prior to storage verify that each package meets the packaging requirements for the contents, check that they have been properly sealed and verify warning labels and all available information have been documented on the outer packaging (barcode labels, handwritten receipts, etc.). Ensure any required paperwork or data entry has been completed. If any of the required information is incomplete, the submitter will be immediately notified of the needed corrections and the item(s) will be placed in a secure correction pending area.

If the submission is correct and complete, it can be placed in permanent storage. The storage location and date the items were placed in storage need to be documented by an electronic tracking system or on the hardcopy evidence receipt.

(a)   (b)

Figure 2.4 Examples of properly sealed items.

Access to evidence receipts and evidence management software should be limited to evidence staff. This information must be retained according to the agency's state retention laws. If a hardcopy receipt is used, it will need to be archived appropriately.

Tracking evidentiary items provides an agency with the statistical data, documentation for audits and information for physical inventories to be conducted. Audits should be conducted quarterly by personnel outside of the evidence staff. Inventories should be performed annually and the results reported to the agency's administration. Additionally, an agency can use the statistical information to determine if the volume of work requires increased staffing and can justify demands for supplies.

Storage

Storage locations will vary depending on the size of packaging and the temperature requirements for the contents. Basic storage areas will need to include the following:

- Shelved general storage area (preferably metal or non-porous shelving)
- Refrigerator unit and freezer unit
- Bulk storage areas
- High-security storage
- Valuables safe
- Secure outside storage

The chart below provides basic guidelines for common items and storage locations.

Storage Area Type	Common Items
General storage shelves	Controlled temperature items
Refrigerator/freezer units	Blood, urine and tissue
Bulk storage	Carpets, TV's, furniture
Outside storage	Bikes, gas-powered tools, transient property
High-security storage	Drugs and weapons
Valuables safe	Currency, counterfeit bills and jewellery

The secure evidence storage areas, evidence vaults, should be housed inside a facility where none of the walls are exterior walls of the building. The building material should have a 2-hour fire protection rating. The evidence vault should not have drop ceilings or windows. The area should be equipped with emergency lighting, backup generator for refrigeration units, a sprinkler system, intrusion and duress alarms and 24-hour video monitoring. Access to the evidence vault and other evidence storage areas should be limited to the evidence staff. All vistors should be required to sign into a log book and be escorted by evidence staff while inside the secure area. Security measures such as key control and electronic door locks are to be used to increase security.

Interior storage locations need to have temperature and humidity control in order to preserve the evidence. Recommended storage area temperatures can be found in (NISTIR 7928) *The Biological Evidence Preservation Handbook* (Ballou et al., 2013).

- Temperature-controlled area: Between 60°F and 70°F with less than 60% humdity
- Refrigerated temperature: 36° F to 46° F with less than 25% humdity
- Frozen temperature: at or below 14° F

High-security vaults that house money, weapons or drugs will have no exterior building access, drop ceilings or windows. If staffing allows, high-security storage should only be accessed when two employees are present. The storage should be monitored by 24-hour survelliance. Additional high-security storage vaults containing drugs should have a negative pressure ventilation system. Due to the health and safety risk of the contents, this area needs to be climate controlled to prevent the growth of dangerous mould and fungus. Valuables such as money and jewellery have to be stored in the high-security area inside a safe. The combination or keys to the valuables safe will always be changed when there is any change in evidence staff personnel.

Exterior storage locations need to be well ventilated, secured with limited access and monitored by alarm or security camera. The exterior area should have shelving that can accommodate oversized items, bicycles and tools. There should be a designated cabinet for the storage of combustibles and staff should be trained on fire safety and prevention.

Organizing any of the storage areas needs to be well thought out and systematic. There are a large number of shelving options and storage bins available but each agency will have unique spacing needs and varying budgets. Due to the nature of the items being stored, non-porous shelves are ideal to prevent contamination. High-density shelving is also available for high-volume needs within limited space. At no time should evidentiary items be permitted to be stored on the floor of a storage area. This practice will reduce tripping hazards and prevent loss or damage to items if there is flooding in the storage area.

Once shelving is in place, the area can be labelled to fit the organizational needs of the contents. For example, small items such as envelopes can be stored in bins by size, then stored in order by case number, going top to bottom and then left to right (Figure 2.5a and b). This allows for easy consolidation of inventory within the same location. Large bulk items can be stored

EV1 (Location name)	EV1	EV2 (Location name)	EV2	EV3 (Location name)	EV3
6 × 9 Envelopes	6 × 9 Envelopes	9 × 12 Envelopes	9 x 12 Envelopes	11 × 14 Envelopes	11 × 14 Envelopes
Bin 1	Bin 6	Bin 1	Bin 6	Bin 1	Bin 6
Bin 2	Bin 7	Bin 2	Bin 7	Bin 2	Bin 7
Bin 3	Bin 8	Bin 3	Bin 8	Bin 3	Bin 8
Bin 4	Bin 9	Bin 4	Bin 9	Bin 4	Bin 9
Bin 5	Bin 10	Bin 5	Bin 10	Bin 5	Bin 10

Figure 2.5 Small items storage in bins by size, then stored in order by case number going top to bottom and then left to right.

in one area and need to have labels clearly visible with the case information (Figure 2.6a and b).

Cold storage areas can range from a small refrigerator and freezer unit to large walk-in refrigerators and freezers. Temperatures of these units should be monitored once a week to ensure they are meeting minimum standards. Similar organization techniques can be used in the cold-storage areas as is used in general storage. Small items can be placed in bins and placed in order by case number.

Employing these tracking and organizational measures, along with proper climate control, will help maintain the integrity of the evidence in the agency's care. Written policies and procedures will create consistency, which will allow an agency to be confident in its practices. Annual audits and inventories will keep the staff and administration apprised of any areas of improvements before they develop into systemic issues. These steps will

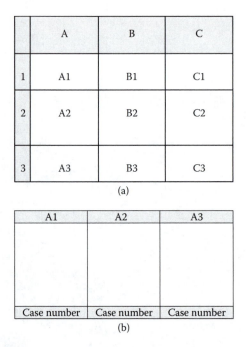

(a)

(b)

Figure 2.6 (a) Shelf labelling configuration large items. Each row of shelves has a unique location label. These shelving areas can be used for larger bags and boxes. (b) Bulk storage shelves with case information clearly visible.

enable the agency to meet its responsibility to maintain an accurate chain of custody and preserve evidentiary items for court.

Reference

Ballou, S. M., Kline, M. C., Stolorow, M. D., Taylor, M. K., Williams, S. R., Bamberger, P. S., Yvette, B., Brown, L., Jones, C. E., Keaton, R., Kiley, W., Thiessen, K., LaPorte, K., Latta, J., Ledray, L. E., Nagy, R., Schwind, L., Stoiloff, S., and Ostrom, B. (2013). *The Biological Evidence Preservation Handbook: Best Practices for Evidence Handlers*. NIST Interagency/Internal Report (NISTIR), 7928, 1–64.

Evidence Management of Fingerprints

3

JACK FLANDERS

Contents

Proper packaging of evidence is crucial and directly related to the successful recovery of latent print evidence. Latent prints are composed primarily of water and are fragile in nature. Latent prints can easily be destroyed by improper packaging. The following guidelines are meant to help protect evidence for the successful recovery of latent prints; however, always follow your agency's Standard Operating Procedures if applicable.

All evidence should be handled as little as possible and in areas that would unlikely be touched. Excessive handling of evidence is an easy way to wipe away or otherwise destroy potential latent prints. Gloves should always be worn when handling evidence for collection and packaging. Gloves help to prevent the investigator/officer from contaminating evidence with their own prints. However, gloves do not offer any protection to the evidence. Evidence should not be allowed to rub up against other items (Figures 3.1 and 3.2).

Documentation

Avoid writing identifying information on evidence until after it has been processed. Instead, place all pertinent information on the packaging. If you must label the item, try placing a tag on or with the item. When information is written on the evidence prior to processing, it could obscure or destroy latent prints. Alternatively, latent print processing chemicals could cause some inks to run potentially destroying more latent prints (Figure 3.3).

Label paper packaging with as much information as possible prior to collecting the evidence. This eliminates contacting the item's surface with the

Figure 3.1 The examiner is holding the object on edges where the object would be less likely to be touched and less likely to contain friction ridge detail.

Figure 3.2 The objects are not packaged correctly and the surfaces would likely rub together during transit and storage. The objects should have been packaged in separate containers.

packaging and potentially writing on top of the item's surface. It should also be clear in case notes what is packaging provided by the agency and what is evidence. This can get confusing with controlled substance cases (Figure 3.4).

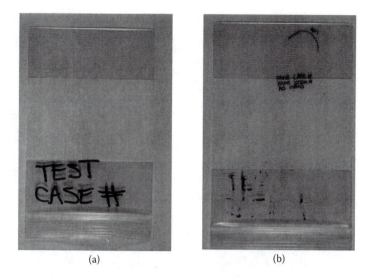

(a)   (b)

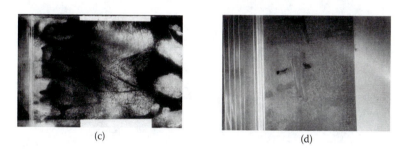

(c)   (d)

Figure 3.3 (a)–(d) The ink from the markings ran during processing, obscuring friction ridge detail. (Courtesy of Ashley Durham.)

Only collect after all necessary documentations (photographs, sketches) have been made. At a minimum, latent print evidence should be documented with:

- Overall, mid-range and close-up photographs
- The location of the item
- The condition of the item (as necessary if wet, contains possible blood, etc.)
- Any processing techniques used
- Sketch and orientation if utilizing lift cards

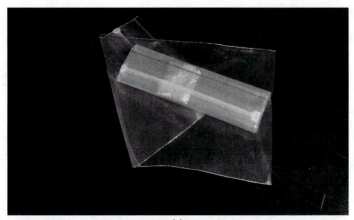

(a)

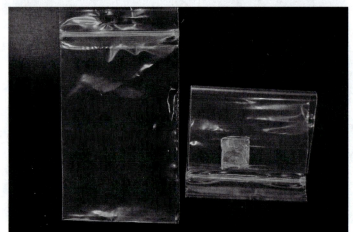

(b)

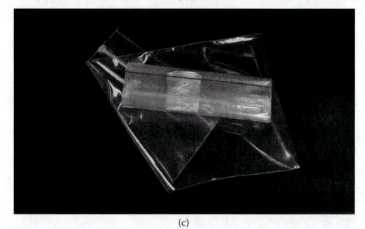

(c)

Figure 3.4 (a)–(c) Multiple plastic layers. Case documentation must be clear to indicate if all of these plastic layers are evidence, or if they were provided by the investigator.

The majority of items can be properly packaged in paper or cardboard which allows the items to breathe. Plastic is often inappropriate especially if the item is moist. Packaging wet items in plastic can cause the item to grow mould which can be a huge detriment to latent print processing. Latent lift cards would be an exception to this.

Place sharp objects such as knives in cardboard boxes or sharps tubes. Zip ties can be used to keep the objects from sliding around in a box, but again make sure to handle the item as little as possible.

Care should be exercised when unloading a firearm and gloves should always be worn. Try to avoid handling smooth areas when possible. Securing the firearm and/or firearm accessories will help to prevent the surfaces from sliding around and destroying potential latent prints. If possible, avoid unloading firearm magazines if the cartridges are to be processed.

Remember, almost any item can contain latent prints, but heavily textured areas and fabrics are far less likely.

Surfaces

There are three main types of surfaces of concern for latent print processing and their packaging needs vary (Table 3.1).

Table 3.1 Surface Packaging Considerations

	Types	Packaging	Considerations
Porous			
	Paper (copy paper, cardstock, etc.)	Envelopes for small amounts; paper bags or boxes for large amounts	
	Cardboard	Envelopes, paper bags, boxes or wrap in paper	
	Unfinished wood	Paper bags, boxes or wrap in paper	
Non-porous			
	Plastic	Paper bags or boxes	Single-item flat pieces of plastic can be packaged in envelopes Avoid packaging items together if possible
	Metal	Paper bags, boxes or wrap in paper for large items	Avoid packaging items together if possible

(Continued)

Table 3.1 (*Continued*)   Surface Packaging Considerations

	Types	Packaging	Considerations
	Glass	Paper bags, boxes or wrap in paper for large items	Avoid packaging items together if possible
	Finished wood	Paper bags, boxes or wrap in paper	Avoid packaging items together if possible
Semi-porous			
	Glossy paper	Envelopes, paper bags or boxes	Treat these surfaces like non-porous; items should not be allowed to rub against one another
Adhesive			
	Tapes	Consider utilizing wax paper, non-stick foil or acetate sheets to line a cardboard box. This will keep the tape from sticking to the packaging	Avoid placing tape on paper surfaces like paper sacks. Do not press the tape down to a surface (both sides of the tape are valuable latent print evidence)
Blood			
	Any of the above surfaces	Paper sacks and cardboard boxes	Make sure any blood evidence has dried prior to final packaging. Avoid plastic packaging and if possible photograph visible ridge detail prior to packaging

Porous

Latent print residue is absorbed into porous surfaces. This allows for easier packaging – most porous surfaces can be packaged in envelopes or cardboard boxes if necessary. If a large amount of paper is considered one item, packaging the paper together will not be detrimental to latent print processing. However, paper or notebook covers that have semi-porous cover or pages should not be packaged in a manner to allow the surfaces to rub together as latent print residue could be on the outer surface.

Porous surfaces that have been wet should be dried prior to final packaging. It is also important to the latent print examiner to document that the surface has been wet. Common latent print processing techniques such as amino acid reagents (ninhydrin, 1,8-Diazafluoren-9-one [DFO] and 1,2-indandedione) are typically ineffective on surfaces that have been wet because amino acids are soluble in water. Once dried, the item(s) can then be packaged in paper or cardboard as normal.

Non-Porous

Latent print residue is not absorbed into non-porous surfaces, but stays on the outside of the surface. Paper bags and/or cardboard boxes are typically utilized for packaging. When non-porous items are packaged together with other items or are not secured in a large container, latent print residue can be destroyed from the surface. The best solution is to package non-porous items separately from other items in their own individual containers. Alternatively, the investigator can use packaging materials at their disposal to create special packaging to fit their needs. For example, if a large number of bottles are collected, cardboard can be cut to create dividers to place inside of a large box that can hold all the bottles. This keeps the bottles from moving around and rubbing against each other (Figure 3.5).

For oversized items, paper or cardboard boxes can be taped together around the entire item; avoid putting pressure on the item's surface when taping and/or sealing.

Figure 3.5 Homemade dividers.

Some agencies have had great success with fuming non-porous items with cyanoacrylate (super glue) prior to packaging in an attempt to preserve any latent print evidence prior to packaging. This should only be attempted by trained investigators. Any visible latent prints should be photographed prior to any processing and over-processing with cyanoacrylate can be detrimental to any further latent print processing.

Latent Lift Cards

Black powder lift cards from crime scenes can be packaged together in envelopes. It is not necessary to use excessive packaging with this type of item. It may be beneficial to package lift cards from different areas in different envelopes. For example, a crime scene may encompass several structures and/or vehicles. The investigator could package the lift cards from one structure in one envelope and from a vehicle in another envelope. This will help to keep all of the lift cards organized.

Do not wrap evidence in plastic or cling wrap to try to preserve latent print evidence – this will likely destroy latent print residue. If visible latent prints are observed, do not place tape over the print as this will also destroy any latent prints. It is important to remember that lifting tape lifts powder from the surface; it is not a reliable method of lifting visible latent print residue.

Adhesive Surfaces

Tape is a commonly encountered item that can be difficult to package. Simply placing tape with exposed adhesive in a paper bag can easily destroy latent prints. The tape will commonly stick to the bag and rip the packaging when removed for latent print processing. Wax paper or plastic acetate sheets can be used to keep the tape from adhering to the packaging. The investigator can either place the acetate sheets or wax paper in a box prior to placing the tape inside, or gently place the tape on the acetate or wax paper, then place the tape inside the box. Paper bags are typically not useful for packaging tape (Figures 3.6 and 3.7).

Surfaces that contain apparent blood can also have special considerations. Again, any items that are wet should be dried prior to final packaging. If possible, photograph any visible latent prints prior to packaging.

Casting materials like Mikrosil can be packaged in paper or cardboard, but should not be stored in prolonged warm environments as this could dry out the material. Make sure to package the casts in a way to prevent other packages of evidence from crushing the casts.

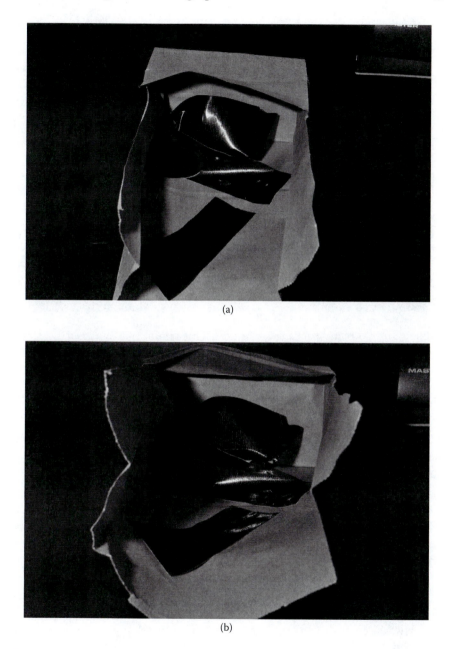

(a)

(b)

Figure 3.6 (a) and (b) Incorrectly packaged duct tape. These two photographs show duct tape sticking to the inside of a paper sack. This is not an appropriate way to package tape as friction ridge detail on the sticky side of the tape can easily be lost.

Figure 3.7 Correctly packaged duct tape. This photograph shows utilization of wax paper as a liner on the inside of a cardboard box. The tape will not adhere well to the wax paper and can easily be removed by a latent print examiner.

Fingerprints in the Digital World

Digital evidence such as latent print photographs or scans should also be packaged correctly. All comparison quality latent print images should be captured in either TIFF or RAW format, not Joint Photographic Experts Group (JPEG). Close-up images of latent prints should always have a scale placed on the same plane as the latent print so that the image can be calibrated to 1:1 size. Images can be saved on a tangible medium such as a CD, DVD, memory card or thumb drive. These items can be sealed in paper, plastic or cardboard. Images can also be submitted to some laboratories by email. Ensure that a secure electronic account is used for these types of submissions. In the United States, the Federal Bureau of Investigation (FBI) can provide law enforcement agencies with secure law enforcement only (LEO) email accounts.

Always remember to check with the laboratory that you use for any special requirements.

Bibliography

Ramotowski, R. (2013). *Lee and Gaensslens Advances in Fingerprint Technology*. Boca Raton, FL: CRC Press.

Texas Department of Public Safety. (2016). *Physical Evidence Handbook*. Retrieved October 11, 2017 from https://www.dps.texas.gov/CrimeLaboratory/documents/PEHmanual.pdf.

Biological Evidence
Collection, Transportation and Preservation

4

NATHALIE ZAHRA

Contents

Biological Evidence

Police investigations rely mostly on items collected from scene of crime (SOC) to use as evidence that an action of crime has been committed. However, these can be used for both the incrimination and exoneration of a person brought forward as a suspect in a criminal case. There are various types of evidences, with physical evidence (such as glass and fibres) and biological evidence (such as blood, semen and hair) being the most reliable. Focusing on the latter, biological evidence gained much of its importance throughout the years with the development of new technology and advances in their sensitivity towards trace evidence.

Giving particular attention to genetic analysis, the development of the PCR technology and use of the short tandem repeat (STR) markers in DNA for human identification revolutionized the field of forensic. This was initially applied to cases such as homicides and sexual assault cases when biological material of good quality and quantity was recovered. However, the further increase in the procedural sensitivity allowed the analysis of samples with limited quantities and qualities to be analysed, i.e. degraded, contaminated or trace samples.

The DNA's practical application is based on the principle that cellular material left on the SOC can be used to extract DNA and generate a DNA profile. This led to the collection and submission of a wider range of exhibits, including those that might contain touch DNA such as clothing and objects used as weapons. The term touch DNA refers to the DNA obtained from epithelia skin cells left behind on objects upon touching (Hess and Haas, 2017; Pfeifer and Wiegand, 2017). This in turn increased the range of offences for which DNA profiling are used to include volume crimes such as burglaries, vehicle crimes, drug cases and counter terrorism.

Dealing with such sensitive samples, it is now even more important to have and follow specific procedures that have been developed and accredited for the collection and preservation of the exhibits. This will ensure the preservation of exhibits from further degradation, contamination or loss in quantity. Both in the United States and in Europe, professional forensic laboratories are required to adhere and be accredited to ISO 17020 and 17025 standards (Horswell, 2016; Kelty et al., 2011).

Training of scene of crime officers (SOCOs) on the different types of evidence, the importance of the evidence, identification and proper collection of items with evidential value according to laboratory procedure is mandatory. It therefore lies within the SOCO responsibilities to preserve the scene, identify key evidence area and types, record and recovery all evidence and package and store evidence.

In this respect, this chapter aims to provide guidelines on the general procedures used for the collection, preservation and transport of the different biological material commonly encountered on an SOC.

Collection and Preservation of Biological Evidence

The first thing that an SOCO needs to consider before attending an SOC is to ensure that all the necessary materials needed for the examination of a scene and collection of biological evidence are available (Pepper, 2010). A list of basic items that might be required during the examination of an SOC is given in Table 4.1. Other more specialized equipment may be required depending on the SOC visited.

Once on the scene, the officer needs first to perform a survey of the scene, decide on the search pattern and the sequence the evidence is going to be collected. As a general rule, the evidence which is most fragile (i.e. evidence that is sensitive to environmental conditions or that is prone to destruction unless recovered) has to be collected and packaged first.

Table 4.1   Items and Reagents That Might Be Needed During a Scene of Crime Investigation

ITEMS

- Protective Personal Equipment (PPE): These include:
  - Gloves (latex, nitrile, cotton)
  - Facemasks (and/or respirators designed to protect against blood-borne viruses and dust)
  - Hair nets
  - Plastic overshoes
  - One-piece disposable suit
  - Safety spectacles or goggles
- Sterile sealed swabs
- Disposable sterile tweezers/forceps
- Selection of plastic tubes and pots
- Sterile disposable plastic pipettes
- Disposable sterile scalpels or razor blades
- Biological hazard bags and sharp bins
- Selection of sizes of tamper evidence or polythene bags
- Selection of sizes of brown paper sacks
- Selection of sizes of cardboard boxes (flat pack)
- Scissors
- Sellotape
- Stapler and staples
- Evidence tape and tags
- Scene of Crime barrier tape
- Small identification labels used during photography
- Pens and indelible markers to write on clear plastics
- Ruler and tape measure
- Plain paper (A4 and A3)
- Thermometer
- Magnifying glass
- Torch
- Fingerprint brushes and selection of fingerprint powders
- Lifting tape with acetate sheet
- Alternative light source (ALS)
- Digital and video camera
- Clipboard
- Crime Scene Investigation forms and necessary laboratory documents

REAGENTS

- Distilled or deionized water (sterile)
- Ethanol for cleaning
- Bleach
- Reagents for presumptive testing of biological stains
- Fingerprint enhancement reagents

Various biological evidences can be encountered, with typical materials being blood, saliva, semen, hair, bone, tissue, fingermarks and hair. While some of these may be clearly visible to the naked eye, others can be in low quantities or colourless making them difficult to see or identify. To target the latter case, chemicals and/or alternative light sources can be used for detection. For example, Luminol is used to detect traces of blood, while Polilight can be used to detect stains of blood, semen and saliva without the need of any chemicals (Miranda et al., 2014; Sterzik et al., 2016). With regards to objects or areas that have been touched, fingerprint agents are usually used to enhance the latent prints. In most cases, DNA can still be recovered following the enhancement treatment (Kumar et al., 2015). However, if touch DNA is a priority, collection of the items is usually based on assumption about where the DNA-containing material is located (Oorschot et al., 2010).

Independent of the type of biological material that might be present at the SOC, the SOCO needs to take some precautionary steps to ensure the preservation of the evidence. Some practical aspects that require appropriate consideration with respect to the collection and preservation of evidence are outlined in the 'Practical Considerations for Collection of Biological Evidence' section. More specific procedures used for the collection of evidence are outlined in the 'Procedures for the Collection and Preservation of Biological Evidence' section. Furthermore, Table 4.2 outlines the procedures that are used for the collection, packaging and storage of the various possible biological samples. All methods outlined in this chapter have to be previously validated by the laboratory before being used on actual samples as they need to ensure the preservation of the sample.

Practical Considerations for Collection of Biological Evidence

The following list gives some practical points that need to be taken into consideration when collecting, transporting and preserving evidence:

- When going to an SOC, ensure you have all the necessary items with you. A list outlining the main items can be found in Table 4.1.
- Officers dealing with the SOC and collection of evidence need to wear proper garments including full-body disposable suits, face masks, hair nets, shoe covers and gloves. This will help to avoid the contamination of the area where biological material can be present. There should be no touching of evidence with bare hands and no talking, sneezing or coughing over evidence. THIS IS PARTICULARLY IMPORTANT WHEN DEALING WITH TRACE AND TOUCH EVIDENCE.

Table 4.2 Biological Evidence Most Commonly Encountered at a Crime Scene and the Procedure Used to Collect and Preserve Them

Biological Evidence	Description of Evidence	Collection Procedure	Packaging Procedure	Storage Procedure
Blood	Blood from a person	• Collection of blood should be done by a qualified medical person. • Collect 2 × 5 mL of blood in an EDTA vacutainer. • Label tube appropriately.	• Store the vacutainers in a sealable bag. • Place in a cool and dry container for transportation.	For short-term and long-term storage, place the sample at 4°C. Do not freeze.
	Liquid blood from scene of crime	• Use a sterile disposable syringe or pipette. • Take up few mL of blood. • Transfer to a sterile 2-mL tubes.	• Label tube appropriately. • Place in a cool and dry container for transportation.	For short-term and long-term storage, place the sample at 4°C. Do not freeze.
	Blood clots	• Use sterile disposable spatula to pick blood clot. • Transfer sample to a sterile tube.	• Label tube appropriately. • Place in a cool and dry container for transportation.	For short-term and long-term storage, place the sample at 4°C. Do not freeze.
	Blood spatter	• For a wet spatter, use a sterile buccal swab to sample the blood. Allow the swab to dry and place back in swab container. • For dry spatter, moisten the buccal swab and use the double swabbing method to take a sample. Allow the swabs to dry and place back in swab container. • For dry spatter, using a spatula to perform the scraping method. Collect the scraping in a paper bag.	• Place the swabs containers or envelope into evidence bags, seal and label appropriately. • Place in a cool dry container for transportation.	For short-term and long-term storage, place the sample at 4°C. Do not freeze.

(Continued)

Table 4.2 (Continued) Biological Evidence Most Commonly Encountered at a Crime Scene and the Procedure Used to Collect and Preserve Them

Biological Evidence	Description of Evidence	Collection Procedure	Packaging Procedure	Storage Procedure
	Items containing blood	• Depending on the nature and the size of the item, use the double swabbing method (for non-porous surfaces), cutting method (for porous surfaces) or the scraping method (for dry stains). • Package the item.	• Place the swabs containers or envelope into evidence bags, seal and label appropriately. • Place in a cool dry container for transportation.	For short-term and long-term storage, place the sample at 4°C. Do not freeze.
Sweat/skin	Sweat from clothing	• To recover biological material from clothing, use the double swabbing method or the cutting method. • For swabs, place them back in the original container. • For cuttings, place them in an envelope.	• Place the swabs containers or envelope into evidence bags, seal and label appropriately. • Place in a cool dry container for transportation.	For short-term and long-term storage, place the sample at 4°C.
	Fingermarks or enhanced fingerprints	• Use the double swabbing method to take a sample from the fingermarks or enhanced fingerprints. • Place the swabs back in their original containers.	• Place the swabs containers or envelope into evidence bags, seal and label appropriately. • Place in a cool dry container for transportation.	For short-term and long-term storage, place the sample at 4°C.

Biological Evidence	Description of Evidence	Collection Procedure	Packaging Procedure	Storage Procedure
Saliva		• Use the double swabbing method to take a sample from the saliva sample. • Place the swabs back in their original containers.	• Place the swabs containers or envelope into evidence bags, seal and label appropriately. • Place in a cool dry container for transportation.	For short-term and long-term storage, place the sample at 4°C.
Bones and teeth		• Recover bone and teeth by using a sterile disposable forceps. • Place the specimen in a sterile plastic container. • Seal container and label appropriately.	• Place in a cool dry container for transportation.	For short-term and long-term storage, place the sample in a cool dry place.
Tissue	Soft tissue	• Use a sterile disposable forceps to pick the tissue. • Place the tissue in a sterile plastic container.	• Promptly cool the tissue for transportation. • Freeze the tissue when possible.	For short-term and long-term storage, place and maintain the sample at −20°C.

(Continued)

Table 4.2 (Continued) Biological Evidence Most Commonly Encountered at a Crime Scene and the Procedure Used to Collect and Preserve Them

Biological Evidence	Description of Evidence	Collection Procedure	Packaging Procedure	Storage Procedure
	Formalin-fixed and paraffin-embedded tissue	• Cut a cross section of the tissue and place in a plastic container.	• Place the container in an evidence bag, seal and label appropriately. • Place in a cool dry container for transportation.	For short-term and long-term storage, place the sample at 4°C.
Semen	Semen from person	Use rape kit to collect all the samples from victim. This should be done by a trained medical professional.	• Place sample in evidence bag, seal and label appropriately.	For short-term and long-term storage, place the sample at 4°C.
	Semen from substrates	• Use the double swabbing method to recover a sample from dry stains. • Place the swabs in original containers. • Use the cutting method to recover the stain from large objects. • Place cutting in an envelope.	• Place the swabs and envelops in evidence bag, seal and label appropriately. • Place in a dry cool place.	For short-term and long-term storage, place the sample at 4°C.
Vaginal fluid	Vaginal fluid from person	Use rape kit to collect all the samples from victim. This should be done by a trained medical professional.	• Place sample in evidence bag, seal and label appropriately.	For short-term and long-term storage, place the sample at 4°C.
Hair		• Using a sterile disposable forceps, carefully pick the hair strands. • Place the hair in a small paper envelope and seal.	• Place the envelope in an evidence bag, seal and label appropriately.	For short-term and long-term storage, place the sample at 4°C.

- All evidence should be documented with notes, photographs, videotape and sketches before collection.
- Every effort has to be made to reduce chemical contamination and eliminate biological contamination coming from other samples and from scene crime officers. Some precautions include individual packaging, use of sterile equipment and change of gloves when dealing with different evidence.
- Exhibits containing liquid samples such as blood and semen stains should be allowed to dry before packaging. When swabbing technique is applied, allow the swab to dry in air without touching other objects. Then store each swab separately.
- The method used to recover biological evidence depends on the state, quantity and condition of biological material. Enough material has to be collected to ensure downstream processing such as DNA analysis, protein and enzyme for toxicological analysis.
- When sampling a stain, a substrate control sample needs to be taken. This is a sample taken from an unstained portion of the object. This control sample should be collected and packaged separately and submitted to the laboratory.
- For packing of items with biological stains, use paper bags and cardboard boxes. Avoid the use of plastic bags as these retain moisture and can speed the degradation of the sample.
- On collection, evidence needs to be sealed and properly labelled with details such as item number, date, time, location, name of collector (badge number) and brief description. On the package also indicate the appropriate storage conditions, i.e. room temperature, fridge or freezer.
- Compile a list of all the items recovered from the SOC. This can be used as a checklist throughout the investigation.
- After collection, samples need to be promptly delivered to the lab for proper storage and analysis. During transportation, the items should be kept in a cool dry environment to prevent damage or further degradation of the sample.
- Prepare any documentation that is required to ensure chain of custody.

Procedures for the Collection and Preservation of Biological Evidence

Various methods can be used for the collection of biological material from different items. For the recovery of body fluids such as blood, semen, saliva and fingermarks, the methods that can be used include the double swabbing method (see 'Double Swabbing Method' section), the cutting method (see 'Cutting Method' section), the scraping method (see 'Scraping Method' section) and the tape lifting method (see 'Tape Lifting Method' section). With hair strands, these can be recovered either with the tape lifting method or picking method (see 'Picking Method' section). Other solid biological material such as tissue or bones, these are usually recovered with the picking method. All the above methods can be used both at the SOC to recover biological material from large non-movable objects or in the laboratory from smaller objects that are submitted for examination.

Double Swabbing Method

Use the double swabbing method to collect dry evidence from medium to large non-porous items such as metal, glass or plastic (Pang and Cheung, 2007). This can also be used for touch DNA from objects (Pang, 2007). The procedure is as follows:

- With gloved hands, moisten the swab with sterile water.
- Brush over the surface containing the dry stain. This will loosen any cell present and rehydrate the cell.
- With a second dry swab, pass over the stain to collect any additional/ remaining cell.
- Air-dry the swabs and place each swab in a separate package.
- Keep swabs in a dry cool place until ready for processing.

Cutting Method

When on an SOC, use this method for stains found on large and porous objects (e.g. fitted carpets, sofas). In a laboratory, the method can be used for stains found on smaller objects that have been submitted to the laboratory for examination, e.g. clothing, cigarette butts and chewing gum. The procedure is as follows:

- Identify the region of interest on the object, i.e. region of the stain.
- If the stain is still wet, allow it to dry before performing this procedure.
- With gloved hands, take out a sterile scalp from its packaging.
- With care, cut around the stain.
- Use sterile forceps to pick up the cutting section and place in a paper envelope.
- Seal the envelope and label the envelope accordingly.
- Store at room temperature.

Scraping Method

Use this method to recover dry material from soft and porous items. The method described below should be used in a controlled environment, i.e.

with no wind or traffic and care should be taken with the scraping to avoid contaminating other evidence. The procedure is as follows:

- Identify the region of interest on the object, i.e. region of the stain.
- If the stain is still wet, allow it to dry before performing this procedure.
- With gloved hands, take out a sterile scalp from its packaging.
- With care, use the scalp to scrape a few milligrams of the dry stain onto a clean piece of paper.
- Fold the paper to secure the scrapings.
- Place the folded paper in a paper envelope and seal.
- Label the envelope accordingly.
- Store at room temperature.

Tape Lifting Method

The following method can be used to collect samples of small dry stains from non-absorbent surfaces. Used for powdered fingerprints or areas suspected of containing touch DNA.

- Identify the region on the object containing the biological material.
- With gloved hands get a sterile lifting tape.
- Place the lifting tape over the stain.
- With the fingerprints, gently press the surface of the tape to ensure contact between the adhesive sides of the tape and object.
- Gently lift the tape off from the object.
- Immediately secure the adhesive side to a clear sterile piece of acetate sheet.
- Place the tape in an envelope, seal and label accordingly.
- Store at room temperature.

Picking Method

The following method can be used for the collection of solid biological material such as hair, tissue or bone fragments:

- Wear gloved hands and get a sterile tweezers out of the packages.
- Pick the biological item using the tips of the tweezers.
- Transfer the material into an envelope or plastic container (depending on the biological material).
- Close the container and seal appropriately.
- Fill in the necessary information on the container.
- For samples such as hair and bone, store at room temperature.
- For samples like tissue, store at –20°C.

Reference Sample Collection

Samples from victims, suspects and individuals that are linked to the SOC should be taken to aid the investigation in eliminating or including potential suspects. The most common non-invasive samples that can be readily taken from individuals are buccal swabs and hair samples. The procedures describing the collection of these two samples are outlined in the 'Taking of a Buccal Swab' and 'Taking of a Hair Sample by Plucking' sections.

Liquid blood can also be taken from individuals; however, since this is considered an intimate sample and the procedure is described as invasive, the collection of the sample has to be done by trained medical personnel. Such procedure is described in the 'Taking of Liquid Blood Sample' section.

Reference samples should always be taken after collection of SOC samples to prevent any possible contamination between the two. Also, throughout the different stages of collection, packing, transportation and processing, the reference biological material should be kept separate from the unknown samples recovered from the SOC.

Taking of a Buccal Swab

- Wear gloves when taking a buccal swab from an individual.
- Always handle the swab from the stick avoiding the contamination of the head area.
- Get a buccal swab out from the packaging.
- Instruct the individual to open the mouth.
- Insert the head of the buccal swab in the mouth and rub the swab head against the inside of the cheeks until wet.
- With a second sterile swab, rub the other side of the inside of the cheeks.
- Allow the swabs to dry for a few minutes.
- Once done, place the swabs back in their original package.
- Place both swabs in an envelope, seal and label appropriately including the details of the individual from whom the buccal swab was taken.
- Proceed to take the buccal swab of the next individual. Change the gloves to prevent cross-contamination.
- Store the sample at 4°C.

Taking of a Hair Sample by Plucking

- Using gloved hands, approach the individual and partition the hair.
- Select a strand of hair and grab the hair from the lower part of the strand closest to the scalp.

- With a rapid movement, pluck the hair. Ensure that the root is attached to the hair.
- Pluck a total of 25 hair strands from around the hair.
- Place the hair strands in a paper wrap.
- Place the paper wrap in a polythene bag and label appropriately.
- Store at room temperature.
- If hair from an intimate location is required, seek a medical professional to take the sample.

Taking of Liquid Blood Sample

- This procedure should be carried out by trained medical personnel.
- Collect the blood in a purple-capped vacuum tube containing the anticoagulant ethylenediaminetetraacetic acid (EDTA).
- Fill up two tubes from each individual.
- Label the tubes appropriately with the donor's details.
- Keep the sample at 4°C until use. Do not freeze.

References

Hess, S., and Haas, C. (2017). Recovery of trace DNA on clothing: A comparison of mini-tape lifting and three other forensic evidence collection techniques. *Journal of Forensic Sciences*, 62(1), 187–191.

Horswell, J. (2016). Accreditation: Crime scene investigators. In *Encyclopedia of Forensic and Legal Medicine*, 2nd Ed., pp. 1–11. Cambridge, MA: Academic Press.

Kelty, S. F., Julian, R., and Robertson, J. (2011). Professionalism in crime scene examination: The seven key attributes of top crime scene examiners. *Forensic Science Policy & Management: An International Journal*, 2(4), 175–186.

Kumar, P., Gupta, R., Singh, R., and Jasuja, O. P., (2015). Effects of latent fingerprint development reagents on subsequent forensic DNA typing: A review. *Journal of Forensic and Legal Medicine*, 32, 64–69.

Miranda, G. E., Prado, F. B., Delwing, F., and Daruge, E. (2014). Analysis of the fluorescence of body fluids on different surfaces and times. *Science & Justice : Journal of the Forensic Science Society*, 54(6), 427–431.

Oorschot, R., Ballantyne, K., and Mitchell, R. J. (2010). Forensic trace DNA: A review. *Investigative Genetics*, 1(1), 14.

Pang, B. C., and Cheung, B. K., (2007). Double swab technique for collecting touched evidence. *Legal medicine* (Tokyo, Japan), 9(4), 181–184.

Pepper, I. K. (2010). *Crime Scene Investigation: Methods and Procedures*. Maidenhead: Open University Press.

Pfeifer, C. M., and Wiegand, P. (2017). Persistence of touch DNA on burglary-related tools. *International Journal of Legal Medicine*. 131, 941–953.

Sterzik, V., Panzer, S., Apfelbacher, M., and Bohnert, M. (2016). Searching for biological traces on different materials using a forensic light source and infrared photography. *International Journal of Legal Medicine*, 130(3), 599–605.

Sexual Assault Evidence Collection Techniques

5

LAURIE CHARLES

Contents

The specialty of forensic nursing is a diverse domain within the field of nursing science. These forensic nurses receive extensive training on a wide range of forensic health-care issues. Sexual assault nurse examiners (SANEs) are a subspecialty within forensic nursing science that cares specifically for patients who were sexually assaulted or who were suspected of being sexually assaulted. SANEs are registered nurses who have received detailed and specialized didactic and clinical training in order to perform medical forensic examinations of patients presenting post-sexual assault or violence (International Association of Forensic Nurses [IAFN], 2015). This detailed training allows SANEs to identify, collect and appropriately preserve biological evidence from patients' bodies and their clothing. Didactic classroom requirements for SANEs may vary but are typically 40 hours of adult/adolescent and 40 hours of pediatric patient-specific classroom training.

Patient-Centered Care

Patient-centered care is vital to the success of the sexual assault examination process. Patients who have been sexually assaulted deserve timely, sensitive medical forensic health care provided by qualified medical personnel (QMP), such as SANEs. In order to provide patient-centered care, patients who report sexual assault should be triaged as a high priority in order to quickly address safety, medical and mental health needs while carefully ensuring privacy of their personal health information. SANEs adjust the process as needed so the patient maintains control over the course of the history and examination. Additionally, patients who were sexually assaulted should always be offered a victim advocate from the local rape crisis center. Through hospital accompaniments, advocates support patients and their families by providing non-judgmental support, finding local resources and assisting with paperwork. Advocates support the patient's decisions and maintain strict confidentiality (The National Center for Victims of Crime, 2012).

Violence Against Women Act

The Violence Against Women Act (VAWA) was a seminal piece U.S. legislation. It significantly increased penalties for repeat offenders and made $800 million available over 6 years for training and program support and development. Since its enactment in 1994, 'there has been as much as a 51% increase in reporting by women and a 37% increase in reporting by men' (VAWA, 2013, para. 10). Funding made available by VAWA established and strengthened services ranging from rape crisis services to SANE programs.

The VAWA 2005 Reauthorization added further compliance mandates. Adult victims are provided sexual assault medical forensic examinations with or without law enforcement involvement. The competent adult patient may wish to seek medical forensic health care and have sexual assault evidence collected and stored for a standard period of time. This allows the patient time to decide if they would like to move forward with the case, at which time she or he can report to law enforcement and the sexual assault evidence is available at the hospital or crime lab (Ledray, 2011).

Federal Rules of Evidence

Federal Rules of Evidence, Article IV Relevancy and Its Limits, Rule 412 prohibits the use of victim's prior sexual behavior in any civil or criminal proceeding with exceptions (Federal Rules of Evidence, 2015a). Exceptions include evidence that source of DNA or other evidence including injuries is someone other than the defendant or if exclusion of evidence would violate the defendant's civil rights (Federal Rules of Evidence, 2015a). The forensic examiner may also complete examinations and collect evidence from suspects of sexual violence.

Role of Examiner

The forensic nurse examiner or SANE is to provide complete medical forensic care to patients who report a history of sexual violence. This care includes obtaining a detailed history of the sexual assault, a comprehensive physical assessment of the patient, a meticulous anal and genital assessment and evidence collection if deemed necessary. The SANE connects the patient to community services, law enforcement and counselling for the patient's ongoing physical and mental health needs as well as legal needs. Additionally, SANEs provide crisis intervention and mental health referrals in a caring, compassionate way that supports the patients regardless of their personal health-care choices (Fehler-Cabral et al., 2011).

Legal Considerations

Sexual assault has significant legal implications. Reporting of suspected child abuse is mandated in all 50 states (Title 42 U.S. Code, 2015). The elderly are also protected with federal and state justice statutes.

Reporting

Reporting requirements of sexual assault or abuse differ from state to state. Adults can choose to involve law enforcement after a sexual assault. The sexual assault or abuse of the elderly or children is mandated to be reported by federal and state statutes. Reporting requirements vary based on state definitions of the terms: 'elderly', 'child', 'sexual abuse' or 'rape'. Different states define age of consent to sexual activity based on age. Check the state statutes for clear definitions.

Competent adult patients are allowed to make their own sexual healthcare decisions, including if they choose to report their sexual assault to the authorities. Adults, including active duty military members, can choose to use the 'non-reporting' method, whereby she or he has a medical forensic examination and evidence collection and that evidence is held either by the hospital or the crime lab for a short time frame (often 2–3 years). In that time, the patient can choose to notify law enforcement and report the sexual assault. The stored evidence kit can then be processed for DNA. If the patient does not report, the evidence can be destroyed (Non-Reporting Sexual Assault Evidence Program, 2017).

Examination Process

The sexual assault examination is a detailed, time- and labour-intensive process that typically takes several hours to complete. Most patients reporting acute (within the last 96 hours) sexual assault-related injuries are treated in emergency departments (EDs). As with any other patient, those who have been sexually assaulted must have a minimum screening assessment to rule out life- or limb-threatening emergency medical conditions. The Emergency Medical Treatment and Active Labor Act (EMTALA) outlines criteria for medical screening examinations (MSEs) requirements (EMTALA, 2011). All patients must have an MSE by QMP (EMTALA, 2011). Healthcare systems should determine through their governing medical board of directors who is capable to complete an MSE on a patient who has been sexually assaulted (Chasson and Russell, 2002).

SANEs can be considered QMPs for patients who have been sexually assaulted. However, if any significant medical conditions are found during the SANE's examination of the patient, the ED physician should also examine the patient prior to evidence collection. Policies outlining the appropriate MSE process should be in place to ensure patients' safety so that emergent medical conditions are not missed.

Consent

Written consent for a sexual assault exam is required over and above that of the usual ED visit. A sexual assault examination includes an assessment of private body areas and, therefore, the patient shall always be able to consent or decline to participate in any part of the examination.

Written Authorization

Written, informed authorization by the adult patient begins with a detailed explanation. Children under the age of 18 years may require authorization by a parent, guardian or legal representative. Many states have adolescent sexual health laws that allow adolescents to consent to their own sexual health care to include sexually transmitted infection (STI) testing, pregnancy testing and birth control without parental consent. Many states also have laws that allow physicians, dentists and psychiatrists to treat adolescents when there is a concern for abuse. Risk management and compliance personnel can assist with written authorization questions regarding the elderly and children.

Consent Is Ongoing

Consent for the sexual assault examination is a fluid process where the patient is allowed to consent or decline any part of the process. If the patient were to decline, the SANE should attempt to discern why the patient is declining. It may be that the patient is embarrassed or does not understand the reasoning for a certain step.

History

After the patient's written authorization is obtained, the SANE documents the patient's history of the assault(s). The history is the single most important part of the sexual assault examination, as there are typically no witnesses. The patient's statement should be a verbatim account using the patient's words in direct quotations. Additionally, the history guides the SANE's examination process; it leads the SANE to the evidence to collect.

The patient's history, if obtained in quotes, is admissible in legal proceedings. Hearsay is not admissible except in certain situations. 'Statements made for medical diagnosis or treatment' can be an exception to the federal hearsay rule (Federal Rules of Evidence, 2015b).

Physical Examination

Life- or Limb-Threatening Injuries

If any life- or limb-threatening conditions are found during the physical examination, the SANE stops the examination and a physician assesses and treats the patient until she or he is stable. Upon stabilization, the SANE continues the forensic physical examination.

Head-to-Toe Assessment

With the patient's ongoing consent, the SANE completes a head-to-toe assessment inspecting and palpating body surfaces. Any injuries are documented, and with the patient's consent, photographed with a digital camera.

Injury Documentation

Injuries are documented utilizing body maps or trauma-grams. The SANE accurately documents injuries using medical forensic terminology. Accurate medical forensic documentation includes color, shape, size and description of injury. Injuries should be documented and photo documented. Some jurisdictions do not allow photographs into legal proceedings due to their potentially graphic nature. Photos should include a full head-to-toe of the patient in the clothing they present; a mid-to-close range face photo; a patient identifier with the name, date of birth, medical record number and date seen. Injuries photos should be taken in threes: a mid-range orientation photo, a near-range photo and a near-range photo with a ruler. Many SANE programs use the American Board of Forensic Odontologists (ABFO) No. 2 ©L-shaped ruler.

Evidence Preservation

While times may vary, most states recommend collecting forensic evidence up to 96 hours post-sexual assault in attempt to collect suspect DNA. Numerous scientific articles show varying timelines of viable DNA evidence collection based on the patient's age, sex and type of sexual contact. One researcher found 'the majority of children with confirmed biological evidence present to a medical facility within 24 hours of assault' (Girardet et al., 2011, p. 237).

Evidence Collection Process

Gloves shall be utilized and changed often to prevent cross-contamination throughout the examination and evidence collection process. It is recommended that the SANE print several pages of the patient's identifier labels, initialing each label and timing the label as she or he collects each item.

Sexual Assault Evidence Collection Kit (KIT)

Most SANE programs store their own kits, but law enforcement brings the kit with them to the hospital in some jurisdictions. Once the seal is broken on the kit, it must remain secure at all times with the SANE or locked in a secure cabinet.

Most kits contain:

- Documentation forms including consent, release of evidence and authorization for payment
- Foreign material bag and foreign matter paper sheet
- Underwear/diaper bag
- Debris envelope (includes cotton-tipped applicators, fingernail scraper and paper)
- Head hair combing envelope, paper and comb
- Pubic hair combing envelope, paper and comb
- Penile/genital/vaginal swab and smear (includes cotton-tipped applicators and glass slide)
- Oral swab and smear (includes cotton-tipped applicators and glass slide)
- Anal swab and smear (includes cotton-tipped applicators and glass slide)
- Known saliva sample (includes cotton-tipped applicators)
- Biohazard label
- A pencil
- Two evidence seals

Clothing

Unfold and place a clean bed sheet on the floor. Remove the foreign material bag and paper sheet from the kit. Unfold the paper sheet onto the clean bed sheet on the floor. Label the edge of the paper sheet with the patient's label. If the patient consents to have his or her clothing collected, have the patient stand in the middle of the paper sheet. While the SANE is holding up a patient gown to preserve privacy, the patient takes off his or her clothing and drops each individual item in a different spot on the paper sheet. The patient puts on the gown and the SANE labels each piece of clothing with a label. The clothing is inspected for tears or stains. The SANE documents each item collected and notes a brief description of the item. Each item is bagged, labelled and sealed individually.

Trace Evidence

Fingernail Scrapings

If the patients report scratching their assailant, fingernail scrapings are obtained. The debris envelope is opened and the folded paper is removed. Inside the paper is a fingernail scraper. The SANE or the patient scrapes or swabs with a cotton-tipped applicator under the fingernails of the patient. The fingernail scraper is placed into the paper and the paper is folded pharmacy bindle style to ensure debris cannot fall out of the paper bindle. The bindle is placed into the debris envelope. The envelope is labelled with the patient's name, signed by the SANE and sealed with another label with the patient's name. This process labelling process is used for all envelopes in the kit.

Debris

Debris found on the patient's body should be collected and can be placed into the debris envelope. If there are fingernail scrapings and foreign debris, two envelopes can be used. Label each envelope appropriately. Document all debris collected. The debris envelope has an anterior and a posterior body diagram. The SANE documents from where the debris was collected and what it is suspected of being (suspect saliva or ejaculate).

Oral Evidence

If the patient reports oral penetration, the SANE collects two swabs from the gum line, under the tongue and the posterior crevices of the mouth. Oral swabs should be collected as soon as the patient describes oral assault, as oral evidence degrades quickly (Girardet et al., 2011). Make a slide smear if necessary. Allow swabs and smear to air dry. Label and seal swabs in the provided boxes inside the kit or put them back into the cotton-tipped applicator sleeves.

Genital Examination

The genital examination should begin with a clear explanation of the examination and evidence collection process, allowing for questions. The patient should choose the exam positions in which she or he will be examined.

Colposcope

Many SANE programs utilize a colposcope to aid in the examination process. A colposcope is a bioptic, lighted, low-powered microscope with a digital camera attachment. Most colposcopes serve a dual examination and documentation purpose. Other secure digital camera systems can be utilized.

Positioning

Supine lithotomy position, where the patients are lying on their back with their feet in supports, is one of the best positions in which to examine patients' genitalia. Children with shorter legs may find the supine frog-leg position more comfortable. Children are lying on their back with their feet together so as their legs are bent like a frog. Supine lithotomy and frog-leg both allow for visualization of the labia majora, labia minora and hymen.

Prone knee-chest position is where the patients are on their knees with their head and shoulders on the bed and their buttocks in the air. This position allows for visualization of the anus, perineum and posterior genitalia. The SANE carefully assesses the patient's emotional and psychological reaction to prone knee-chest positioning, as it may be traumatic for the patient to be positioned in such a way. If so, the SANE utilizes another examination position.

Female External Genitalia

The genitalia examination begins with inspection of the inner thighs, groin, mons and labia majora. The aforementioned areas are carefully palpated to assess for point tenderness. Injuries or point tenderness are documented on the appropriate body map and photographed. The labia are separated in order to visualize the inner labia majora and minora. The examiner carefully grasps the labia majora and pulls traction (labial traction) towards the patient's feet to tunnel the genitalia. This allows inspection of the female external genitalia without instrumentation and does not cause pain, unless the patient is already injured. The SANE carefully monitors the patient to ensure her comfort during this process. Photos are typically taken with the use of a foot pedal camera shuttle.

Pubertal versus Prepubertal

The hymen of a prepubertal girl is unestrogenized and is therefore tender. Any contact of the hymen can be extremely painful and should be avoided. Intravaginal instrumentation should not be completed on a conscious prepubertal girl. Labial traction allows visualization into the vaginal vault without intravaginal instrumentation. Prepubertal children typically can tolerate prone knee-chest position easily to allow a thorough examination of their genitalia. Evidence can be collected via cotton-tipped applicators pre-moistened with sterile water or saline. Some jurisdictions require the use of a swab and smear, so a smear can be made with the two applicators. Label each slide with pencil to include patient's name, date of birth, date of exam, examiner's initials and the orifice. Allow swabs and smear to air dry. Label and seal swabs in the provided boxes inside the kit or put them back into the cotton-tipped applicator sleeves.

Vaginal Evidence Collection

Pubertal girls have estrogenized hymens that are non-tender, therefore vaginal instrumentation with a speculum can be tolerated. Sterile water or saline is used to lubricate the speculum prior to insertion. The SANE visualizes the vaginal walls and the cervix and uses at least two cotton-tipped applicators to swab the vaginal vault, posterior fornix and cervix. Label each slide with pencil to include patient's name, date of birth, date of exam, examiner's initials and the orifice. Allow swabs and smear to air dry. Label and seal swabs in the provided boxes inside the kit or put them back into the cotton-tipped applicator sleeves.

Male Genitalia Evidence Collection

Examination of the male genitalia begins with inspection and palpation, assessing for trauma. Injuries and point tenderness are noted on the body map. Two cotton-tipped applicators are pre-moistened with sterile water or saline. The SANE swabs the shaft of the penis, around the base and under the foreskin, if applicable. Care is taken to ensure the applicators do not touch the urinary meatus. All are labelled appropriately.

Anal Examination and Evidence Collection

The anal examination may be completed in the prone knee-chest position or supine knee-chest position where the patients are lying on their back with their knees pulled up to their chest. Both positions have the potential to make the patient feel vulnerable and uncomfortable so care should be taken to ensure safety and comfort at all times. Prone and supine knee-chest positions allow the anus to dilate, thereby facilitating visualization of the anal cavity. Documentation of injury should be completed via body map and photographs.

Two pre-moistened, cotton-tipped applicators are used to swab around the anal folds. A smear is made if applicable in your jurisdiction. Label each slide with pencil to include patient's name, date of birth, date of exam, examiner's initials and the orifice. Allow swabs and smear to air dry. Label and seal swabs in the provided boxes inside the kit or put them back into the cotton-tipped applicator sleeves.

Release of Evidence

Once the patient examination is complete and all photo and written documentation is complete, the evidence is sealed. Clothing items too large to be placed in the kit are individually bagged in brown paper bags and labelled as previously described. Each clothing bag is placed into one large bag which is sealed and labeled.

The kit is sealed with the two evidence seals. The SANE signs from the kit to the seal to the kit. Tampering is easily identified if the signature is not aligned. If there are clothing bags, the kit is labelled 'One of Two' and the clothing is labelled 'Two of Two' to ensure all handlers of the evidence are aware the two go together. Some SANE programs store the evidence until law enforcement can arrive to collect the kit. Others release each kit individually to law enforcement. Either option is viable as long as chain of custody is maintained.

Chain of Custody

Chain of custody documents each person who has had access to the evidence. The SANE opens the kit and seals it back up with the evidence enclosed within. She or he hands the sealed evidence to law enforcement. Both the SANE and law enforcement sign and date the chain of custody form. Chain of custody must be maintained from the SANE to law enforcement to the crime lab to prevent evidence tampering and ensure evidence admissibility in legal proceedings.

References

Chasson, S., and Russell, A. (December 2002). Do SANE examinations satisfy the EMTALA requirement for "medical screening"? *Journal of Emergency Nursing, 28*, 593–595. doi:10.1067/men.2002.129937

Emergency Medical Treatment and Active Labor Act, 42 U.S. Code §1395dd (e)(1) (Cornell School of Law, 2011).

Federal Rules of Evidence, Article IV. Relevance and its limits U.S.C.A. §412 (Cornell University Law School, 2015a). Retrieved from https://www.law.cornell.edu/rules/fre/Rule_412.

Federal Rules of Evidence, Rule 803 Exceptions to the rule against hearsay U.S.C.A. §803 (Cornell University Law School, 2015b). Retrieved from https://www.law.cornell.edu/rules/fre/Rule_803.

Fehler-Cabral, G., Campbell, R., and Patterson, D. (December 2011). Adult sexual assault survivors' experiences with Sexual Assault Nurse Examiners (SANEs). *Journal of Interpersonal Violence*, 26, 3618–3639. doi:10.1177/0886260511403761

Girardet, R., Bolton, K., Lahoti, S., Mowbray, H., Giardino, A., Isaac, R., Arnold W, Mead B., and Pass, N. (2011). The collection of forensic evidence from pediatric victims of sexual assault. *Pediatrics*, 128, 233–238.

International Association of Forensic Nurses. (2015). Sexual assault nurse examiner (SANE) education guidelines. In K. Maguire (Ed.), *Sexual Assault Nurse Examiner (SANE) Education Guidelines* (pp. 3–9, 35–58). Elkridge, MD: Author.

Ledray, L. (2011). Sexual violence: Victims and offenders. In V. A. Lynch and J. B. Duval (Eds.), *Forensic Nursing Science* (2nd ed., pp. 380–396). St. Louis, MO: Elsevier Mosby.

The National Center for Victims of Crime. (2012). *What Is a Victim Advocate?* Retrieved from https://victimsofcrime.org/help-for-crime-victims/get-help-bulletins-for-crime-victims/what-is-a-victim-advocate-.

Non-Reporting Sexual Assault Evidence Program. (2009). *Texas Department of Public Safety*. Retrieved from https://www.dps.texas.gov/crimelaboratory/nrsa.htm.

Title 42 U.S. Code, §13031 Child Abuse Reporting Chapter 132 Subchapter IV U.S.C.A. §Chapter 132 (Cornell University Law School, 2015).

The Violence Against Women Act (VAWA) renewal passes the House and Senate and signed into law. (2013). *Violence Against Women Act*. Retrieved from http://nnedv.org/policy/issues/vawa.html.

Evidence Management Best Practices in Medicolegal Death Investigation

6

JASON WIERSEMA, MICHAL PIERCE,
ALLISON WOODY AND
MICHELLE SANFORD

Contents

Medicolegal death investigation pertains to the process of investigating the circumstances of a person's death for the purpose of determining and/or certifying the most accurate cause and manner of death. This process involves activities at the death scene, in the morgue and in the forensic laboratory and often begins with the medicolegal death investigator (MLDI) at the scene of the death. Careful management of evidence, including the body of the deceased, is imperative to the success of the process. There is significant variability in the medicolegal process from state to state or even country to country; however, temporary possession of the deceased person(s), associated evidence and personal effects, and transport of the decedent for postmortem examination are generally part of the process. While in the possession of the medicolegal entity, items of evidence may be separated from the deceased for laboratory testing (i.e. blood and tissue specimens, trace evidence), for analysis by subject matter experts (i.e. bone, insect specimens) or for archiving of items that may or may not inform the cause or manner of death (i.e. property or clothing items). The effectiveness of the process by which a jurisdiction acquires and possesses these items of evidence and maintains their provenience through the entire process impacts the success of the overall investigation.

In addition to cause and manner of death certification, identification of previously unidentified decedents and maintenance of the identification of those whose identity is known are core components of the medicolegal death investigation process. Circumstances of death may separate decedents from identifying information and/or the MLDI is often left with no prior knowledge of a deceased person's identity. For this reason, it is best practice to manage a deceased body as an item of evidence and to apply evidence management principles throughout the medicolegal process including but not limited to: retrieval of the decedent from the death scene; storage prior to and after examination; during the postmortem examination; and during release of the decedent to family.

This chapter serves as a guideline of evidence management best practices for the medicolegal investigation of individual fatalities as well as multiple/mass fatality incidents. The best practices described pertain to evidence collected by MLDIs and/or other key personnel directly involved in the medicolegal death investigation process such as forensic pathologists, forensic anthropologists, forensic entomologists and forensic laboratory personnel. This chapter then discusses the application of these best practices in both daily medicolegal death investigations and in the multiple/mass fatality context but first provides a basic overview of the death investigation system in the United States.

The Medical Examiner/Coroner System in the United States

The medicolegal death investigation system in the United States is complex and variable. The overall management of the process is carried out by the government, rather than a private function, and operates independently of the mortuary process (which is generally a private function). Some states, generally those that are geographically smaller, operate a central state coroner or medical examiner's office that manages scene and morgue operations for an entire state via a single agency (sometimes with multiple locations). Some states with state coroner or medical examiner's offices have a network of district offices that operate under a state agency umbrella. Other states operate county coroner or medical examiner's offices which are independent of one another and of the state government. There are also states that operate some combination of these strategies.

The range of qualifications among medical examiners and coroners is vast. Coroners are elected or appointed officials, who in many jurisdictions are not required to have either medical or forensic training or experience. The term medical examiner generally implies that an appointed medical doctor conducts postmortem examinations for a particular jurisdiction, but many jurisdictions do not require the physician to have specialized training or certification in forensic pathology. Other, typically larger, jurisdictions require that their medical examiners maintain certification in anatomical, clinical and/or forensic pathology.

Regardless of the strategy a particular state employs, the medicolegal entity is responsible for investigating deaths that meet a particular state's laws and jurisdictional parameters. In general, the fatalities that require medicolegal investigation are unexpected and/or unexplained deaths. Within the United States, the manner of death on a death certificate will typically be categorized as one of five manners: natural, accident, suicide, homicide or undetermined. Examples of some of the deaths that should incorporate a medicolegal death investigation include those involving apparent suspicious circumstances or an intentional act, drug overdoses, firearm-related and motor vehicle accidents.

From place to place, jurisdictions vary in the array of services they provide. Some conduct their own death scene investigations with MLDIs, whereas others conduct postmortem exams and contract the scene and transport components to external or private entities. Laboratory analysis also varies between jurisdictions. Larger offices often maintain their own laboratory facilities, whereas others contract laboratory analysis to external entities. Generally, there is a correlation between the size and complexity of a medicolegal operation and the magnitude and complexity of the evidence management processes it employs. Regardless of the great variety in medicolegal death investigation in the United States, proper management of the deceased including any associated evidence, property and/or specimens taken from the body are common to all systems. Additionally, in spite of the variety seen throughout the United States, the following evidence management best practices are recommended for the success of medicolegal death investigations for any medicolegal entity.

Evidence at the Medicolegal Death Scene

The goals of the medicolegal scene investigation are 1) to reconstruct the events leading to a person's death via consideration of the scene as well as medical, social and psychiatric histories and medications, and 2) to confirm the identity of the deceased person. Each of these goals is described below with specific reference to the management of evidence that informs them.

Again, it is best practice for management of a death scene to regard the body as an evidentiary item and thus to apply the same level of control over the body as is applied to other traditional items of evidence (e.g. blood, fingerprints, gunshot residue, etc.).

Evidence Collection by the MLDI

A core function of the MLDI is to generate a detailed written and photographic record of the activities and health status of the decedent, the location within which a deceased person is found and the relationship of the decedent to items in his/her environment at the time of death. This record reconstructs the events and circumstances associated with a person's death and, in combination with postmortem examination findings, informs the ultimate certification of the cause and manner of death and decedent identification.

The responsibility for handling and management of the body itself and any personal effects should be that of the MLDI or the medicolegal entity until the final disposition occurs, while the remainder of the death scene typically falls under law enforcement jurisdiction. Some examples of exceptions are prescription medications found at the scene that may inform the cause and manner of death, and in some cases, illicit substances that are not readily identifiable. These items are often collected and inventoried as evidence by the MLDI to facilitate toxicological analysis.

The evidence chain of custody (including the body, medications, personal effects and other evidence) starts at the death scene. In situ photographs of these items initiate this process, documenting the presence, location and condition of each piece of evidence pertaining to the cause and manner of death and decedent identification (Figure 6.1). The documentation of pertinent

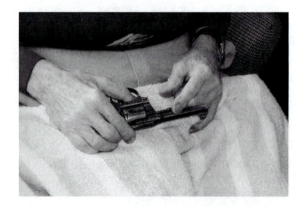

Figure 6.1 It is best practice to photograph items of evidence in situ prior to removal.

negative findings is also part of this process, which is the absence of expected evidence (e.g. turned-out pant pockets with a missing wallet).

Once the body is located, and its location within the scene documented, a head-to-toe inspection of body for evidence, personal effects and trauma should follow. All pockets should be searched, and the entire body patted down to detect items associated with the body. All items of evidence should be photographed and documented in situ, and care should be taken to avoid disruption of evidence prior to transport. After photo documentation, evidence is collected, or left in place, in a manner that best protects the evidence for future examination and testing. Depending on the nature of the evidence or the preferences of the receiving laboratory, items of evidence may be collected for laboratory submission or preserved in situ for analysis at the morgue. For example, after detailed photography, the hands of homicide victims or individuals with possible firearm injuries are sealed within paper bags to ensure that trace evidence remains in place for collection at the morgue. In either case, the MLDI initiates a written record of the type, provenience and management of evidence at the scene for the evidence being collected and transported to the medicolegal entity/office or being released to law enforcement or family on scene.

At the conclusion of the on-scene examination and prior to transport, the body or body parts should be placed in a clean, previously unused body bag (Figure 6.2). The zippers of the bag should be sealed and the seal labelled with identifiers (e.g. specific case number, date of scene investigation and/or MLDI name) if items of evidence are left in place or if there is potential for trace evidence such as gunshot residue or suspect DNA to be present (Figure 6.3); all items of evidence should be properly labelled for maintaining chain of custody and the body inside a sealed body bag is no exception. On-scene trace

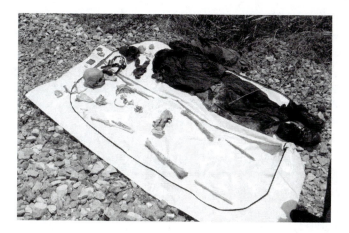

Figure 6.2 Human skeletal remains arranged in anatomical order in a clean, previously unused body bag.

Figure 6.3 Plastic zip tie used to seal zippers of body bag and labelled with specific case number, date of scene investigation and name of the MLDI.

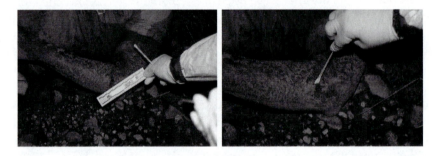

Figure 6.4 Typical labelling and collection of trace evidence from a decedent. Note the scale labelled with case number, date and collector's initials precedes sample collection.

evidence collection may be performed when transport/handling may compromise its later collection. This process should be performed in personal protective equipment (PPE) that protects the MLDI from pathogen exposure while preventing the contamination of the decedent and/or associated evidence with external evidence. PPE for the typical death investigation is minimal, often limited to latex gloves. However, there are scenes that require additional PPE, including appropriately fit-tested N-95 masks, shoe covers and protective sleeves to prevent contamination. Trace evidence collection at the scene may require additional PPE to prevent contamination. Additional PPEs may include hair covers, shoe covers, aprons/gowns and/or polypropylene coveralls.

All trace evidence collected from the body at the scene should be photographed before and after collection, and then sealed in evidence bags prior to transport (Figure 6.4). Transport of the body by the medicolegal entity (rather than an external entity) is preferable from an evidence management perspective because it allows for the maintenance of chain of custody, as the decedent remains in the custody of the medicolegal entity from the scene to the morgue. It is also preferred for sealed body bags, especially if sealed for the purpose of preserving possible trace evidence, to remain sealed during transport and it is best practice for the coroner or medical examiner who performs the exam to be present when the seal is broken. Each trace evidence item collected from the body should be sealed in an evidence bag labelled with the case number, item number and a description of the item as well as its origin, the collector's initials and the date collected. If gunshot residue is collected, the collection should precede tape lifts and other procedures that may disrupt the residue. A control sample should be collected from both gloved hands of the collector for comparison to the samples collected from the decedent. Collection should be administered with gunshot residue stubs, and each stub should be sealed independently, but may then be transported collectively; pre-packaged gunshot residue collection kits are readily available and easy to purchase from various sources for this purpose.

Decedent Identification

Identification of the deceased is a core component of medicolegal death investigation that can cause catastrophic problems with the overall investigation if ignored or managed poorly and is easy to over-complicate without a sound, standardized strategy. Identification of a deceased person involves the comparison of data/information obtained from the decedent (postmortem data) to information collected during life from the person who is believed to be the decedent (antemortem data). Thus, the identification process requires, with few exceptions, prior knowledge of who a person might be. This prior knowledge can take the form of any of a variety of information types including direct identifying information (photo identification, witness statements), contextual information (address of the death, name of person to whom a vehicle is registered, scars/marks/tattoos) or 'scientific' information (radiographs, DNA, fingerprints, etc.). In other words, prior knowledge enables the medicolegal entity to pursue the antemortem information needed to identify a decedent. Without prior knowledge, the medicolegal entity has no means to conduct a meaningful search for antemortem data. Unnecessary separation of potential identifying information is a byproduct of poor scene investigation and is often irreversible once it has happened.

Manipulation and/or movement of the body should be limited to the medicolegal entity or MLDI on scene, and care should be taken to ensure that the relationships between the decedent and associated identifiers remain intact, if possible, or are documented photographically if separation is unavoidable (Figure 6.5). This is made more important in the mass fatality context when the recovery context may be the only source of prior knowledge available.

Figure 6.5 Note the decedent's wallet in the back pocket. The wallet contains an ID which provides the type of antemortem prior knowledge that is required for identification.

Ancillary Services at the Death Scene

Anthropology

Some cases necessitate the involvement of special expertise to ensure the appropriate preservation of certain evidence types. The expertise of the forensic anthropologist is often sought at medicolegal death scenes involving bone exposure and/or significant skeletal trauma. Forensic anthropological assistance can be valuable in ensuring that remains are collected completely, in distinction of bone from other material, and in the recognition of inflicted skeletal trauma in heavily damaged remains. Anthropological site recovery methods are ideal for the recording and maintenance of provenience of items in relation to one another, and are thus well suited for the detection and recovery of evidence at the death scene. Death scenes involving scattered human remains (skeletal or otherwise) often require systematic searches of large areas designed to detect human remains among other material, and also to systematically eliminate areas that have been searched. The circumstances of a particular scene will dictate the search method employed. Simple line searches are best suited for large search areas (Figure 6.6). Large groups, preferably with some knowledge of the medicolegal death investigation process and/or proper search and recovery techniques (often multidisciplinary), should line up single file and progress slowly across a landscape, flagging items (evidence or human remains) along the way without moving them. It is advisable to halt the group in their respective locations as individual searchers locate possibly evidentiary items. There are a variety of other search methods that can be employed depending on the circumstances of the

Figure 6.6 Typical line search strategy for large area searches. Items should be flagged during search and picked up later following photography. Mapping can be conducted post-recovery using the flags that were placed to mark the found location of possible evidentiary items.

scene. For example, searches intended to locate buried remains may require the use of metal probes or ground-penetrating radar to detect soil variation. Regardless of the method employed, once the search is complete, evidence and human remains should be mapped to generate a record of the relationship of each item to every other item and to a datum. The datum should be an item or a feature that can be expected to remain in place as a reference point in the event that the anthropologist or investigator returns to the scene at a later date. A site map can range in detail and complexity from an informal hand-drawn map to one developed electronically via total station or GPS. If multiple maps are generated by independent agencies, it is a best practice to ensure that the data/locations are consistent between maps. Each item identified on the site map should be assigned a unique number or some other designation such that spatial relationships can later be identified. The anthropologist should also identify duplication of skeletal elements, inconsistent morphology between elements or other characteristics that may necessitate the assignment of additional case numbers and separate packaging on the scene. If there is visible or potential commingling of human remains at the scene, it is best practice to map and collect human remains that are not physically attached to one another separately. Their provenience on the map will enable re-association at a later date if needed.

Entomology

Insects and related arthropods can provide a variety of different types of information related to the death investigation including but not limited to: cause of death information (e.g. identification of insects responsible for sting allergy), and the estimation of time of death through examination of post-mortem feeding insects and tools for identification through the extraction of decedent DNA from insect specimens (e.g. maggots and blood feeding insects). The collection of these specimens at the scene is optimal as it reduces the complications associated with cooler storage and allows for the collection of the older life stages that migrate away from the body and are less likely to be collected with the body for transport to the morgue.

Specimens should be collected from areas of insect activity, particularly those that may be associated with potential underlying trauma (Byrd et al., 2010). Representative specimens should be taken with an emphasis on obtaining representatives of the oldest/most developed life stages, keeping in mind that the oldest life stages may be found around the decedent at the scene and not directly on the body (e.g. pupae and empty pupal cases; Figures 6.7 and 6.8).

Figure 6.7 Once fly larvae complete feeding on the body they will migrate away from the body to form the pupa. Outdoors the larvae may burrow into the soil and the migrating larvae, pupae and empty pupal cases (exuvia) may be found by digging into the soil under and adjacent to the body.

Figure 6.8 Once fly larvae complete feeding on the body they will migrate away from the body to form the pupa. Indoors migrating larvae, pupae and pupal cases (exuvia) may be found in carpeting and under clothing or debris near the decedent.

Special collecting equipment and vials can be useful in some circum-stances but are generally not necessary (Figure 6.9). Specimens collected from different locations should be kept separate in labelled containers and contain information about the case, the collection location and time of col-lection (Figure 6.9). Additionally, known predatory beetles and predatory fly larvae should be kept separated from other specimens when observed to be collected together. Each sample is then divided into two representative portions with one portion preserved to establish insect age and the other reared to subsequent older life stages to facilitate and confirm identification. Preservation of soft-bodied insects and larvae should occur via hot water kill followed by placement in 70% ethanol as soon as is practical following col-lection to ensure that the specimens represent those found on the body at the time of collection. Preservation time is critical to the calculation of time of colonization (TOC) for postmortem interval (PMI) estimation and should be recorded along with scene temperature, characteristics of the scene that might alter local temperatures on the body (e.g. direct sun or shade), maggot mass temperatures and temperature modifying mechanisms such as thermo-stat settings indoors. Specimens collected for rearing should be maintained

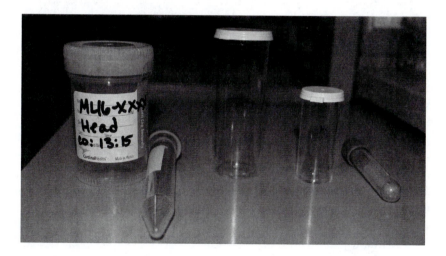

Figure 6.9 Specialized collection vials are not required for collection of insect specimens and can be accomplished with many of the container types found in the morgue. Liquid specimens should be maintained in thread sealed containers (on left) to prevent leakage of liquid. Specimens can be temporarily stored in snap-cap vials (white caps on right) as they are easy to use and inexpensive. Longer term storage of preserved specimens can be accomplished with specimen/blood tubes that are either uncoated or coated with ethylenediaminetetraacetic acid (EDTA) (grey top on right). Specimens should be collected and maintained in separately labelled vials that indicate the case number, location of collection and time of collection. The time of preservation and rearing can be added to the label later when these events take place.

in cool, shaded conditions to minimize growth and stress on the specimens until the rearing container can be established. All samples are maintained separately throughout the collection, processing and rearing process with a minimum labelling requirement of case number, collection location, time of collection and time of preservation or rearing.

Management of Evidence in the Morgue

Autopsy Collection

Collection, packaging and transport of evidence for laboratory analysis must always be carried out in accordance with standard operating procedures (SOPs), no matter if the testing laboratory is in-house or off-site. Improperly collected or packaged evidence could result in the laboratory rejecting the sample or, at the very least, delay the testing. Therefore, SOPs should be written only after consulting with the associated laboratory about their requirements for submission. Furthermore, an incomplete chain-of-custody record could lead to the authenticity of the evidence itself being questioned, which subsequently may lower the probative value of the test results when presented in a court of law. The following is a description of the most common categories of evidence collected for laboratory analysis and is by no means all-encompassing.

A decedent's bodily fluids or tissue samples may be collected in the morgue during the postmortem examination for toxicological analysis to assist in determining cause of death if drugs or alcohol are suspected to be involved. Fluid or tissue may also be sent for DNA analysis, to serve as the decedent's reference sample when identification by DNA is warranted. In each of these scenarios, the collector should be mindful of the different types of tubes for collection (Figure 6.10). Blood, in particular, requires a certain colour of tube top for each type of testing. Purple top tubes contain the necessary preservative for blood samples being sent for DNA, while grey top tubes contain a different preservative used for blood alcohol and drug testing in the toxicology laboratory. Red top tubes have no preservative and are used for serologic testing. After collection, the tubes must be labelled, at the very least, with the case number, source of blood (e.g. 'femoral blood'), date of collection and decedent's name (if known). Other fluids and tissues can be collected in appropriately sized, preservative-free plastic containers with screw tops. The same rules for labelling apply.

For homicide cases that involved direct contact by the perpetrator, trace amounts of DNA may have been deposited on the decedent by the perpetrator during the incident. Therefore, swabbings of areas of potential contact are collected for DNA analysis. A good example is a neck swabbing in a manual strangulation case. In suspected sexual assault cases, swabbings are typically

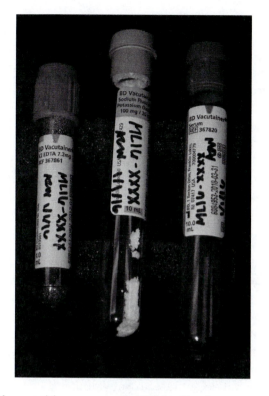

Figure 6.10 Tubes used for postmortem fluid collection.

collected from the vaginal, anal or oral cavities for DNA analysis, or wherever penetration is suspected. If kissing or fondling of other body parts is suspected, such as around the breast area, those areas may be swabbed as well. Two swabs should be used together to swab areas of the body. Some agencies use dry swabs, some moisten swabs with sterile water, and some use a combination of both dry and wet swabs. Care should be taken to keep all swabs separated by collection location, so as not to cross-contaminate. All swabs should be packaged separately in labelled swab boxes suitable for air drying. Labels should include case number, decedent name, date of collection and area of the body from which the swab was taken (e.g. 'vaginal swabs').

Projectiles or bullet fragments recovered from the body may be important to the investigation, specifically when determining the type of firearm that was used to shoot the decedent. These can be picked up with a clean set of tweezers and placed in an appropriate sized, previously unused container such as a small envelope or bag. The collector should not attempt to label or otherwise mark a projectile directly, as this may cover up significant markings. Rather, the envelope should be labelled with all pertinent information.

Foreign hairs, fibres and paint chips all serve as potential trace evidence that may be collected from the decedent's body or clothing. These items should be collected using a clean set of tweezers and placed separately in labelled envelopes. Alternatively, tape lifts of this evidence is an acceptable method of collection. Gunshot residue is another form of trace evidence, but it is not always visible to the naked eye. Therefore, areas of the body or clothing suspected of having gunshot residue are 'stubbed' for it and sent to the laboratory. Special carbon-coated adhesive stubs should be used for this purpose. The outer, plastic cover of the stubs should be labelled with the usual information, including location of collection. Pre-packaged gunshot residue collection kits are available and easy to purchase for this purpose.

It is acceptable for the primary evidence containers (tubes, stubs and envelopes or bags) to be placed in secondary packaging, such as larger paper envelopes or plastic bags. Biohazard specimen bags are encouraged when packaging bodily fluid or tissue containers. Paper bags or envelopes are preferred for packaging body swab boxes to prevent fungus growth. In any case, outer packaging must have a proper seal. The purpose of the seal is to demonstrate the evidence has not been tampered with prior to laboratory processing. Packages can either be heat sealed or sealed with tape. A seal is not complete without a signature or initials of the personnel packaging the item(s). Many forensic agencies and laboratories require a date to be placed over the seal, in addition to the signature or initials.

The chain of custody accompanying each item of evidence collected in the morgue starts with the person responsible for collecting the evidence. Entries continue with all receiving and transport personnel in the chronological order of handling. Minimum standards for chain-of-custody information include name and agency of personnel and the date of transfer. If an item is transferred to a location temporarily, this must also be entered in the chain of custody. While the time of transfer assists with capturing the extent of accountability, not every agency requires the time to be recorded for each transfer. If a forensic agency utilizes a laboratory information management system to generate a chain of custody, security measures must be in place to ensure entries are not erroneously removed or altered. While electronic chains of custody have certain advantages in terms of efficiency, they are equal in merit to hand-written chains of custody, as long as the rules of transfer are followed. Again, a missing or incomplete chain of custody can devalue the evidence.

Anthropology

The forensic anthropologist may be asked to conduct specialized analysis post-autopsy that involves evidence management. Specimens examined by the anthropologist may either be extracted by the anthropologist or pathologist assigned to the case. Extracted specimens should be placed in containers labelled with the case number and transferred directly to the custody of the anthropologist. Specimens should not be labelled directly to prevent disruption of markings of investigative value. Cartilage specimens should be preserved in a 10% formalin solution and may require manual processing to remove unwanted soft tissue and expose underlying cartilage. Unintended markings made to cartilage during manual processing should be acknowledged in the anthropologist's notes. Skeletal specimens may require chemical processing to remove unwanted overlying soft tissue. Care should be taken to avoid damage during processing due to excessive or variable heat, or over-use of detergent. The anthropologist should maintain detailed bench notes that chronicle all anthropological methods applied, their anthropological findings and interpretations, as well as all processing methods employed. Care should be exercised during the analysis phase to ensure that specimens retain their case number by keeping them physically separate from other specimens and maintaining clear case number labelling. If a case requires prolonged examination, the remains should be physically isolated from remains associated with other cases. Following analysis the anthropologist will either return the specimen to the decedent or archive it as evidence. Storage of archived anthropological specimens should occur in a secure facility with a detailed log of access.

Entomology

The same rules that apply to laboratory evidence apply to entomological specimens with a few exceptions. One of these exceptions is in rearing of live insect specimens. Preparation of larval food (e.g. small portions of frozen beef liver) saves time and standardizes the rearing process. Labelling and tracking of specimens into and out of the insect growth chamber with the use of a log ensures that samples are not mixed or lost. The log can also be used to track key life history events such as pupation and emergence of the flies for use in the report. Preservation and storage of live reared insects prior to pinning and mounting is most easily accomplished with a standard freezer. Insect pins can be purchased from a scientific or entomological supply. Many flies reared from death investigations will be a size 0 pin and some will require pointing. Pinning should be performed right out of the freezer to ensure flexibility and to incur the least amount of damage to each specimen. Pinning and mounting follows standard entomological procedures (Espeland et al., 2010) with the pin directed to the right of the midline through the thorax of the insect. Some insect species, such as male flesh flies (Sarcophagidae), may require preparation of the terminalia for examination by a taxonomic expert. Preparation of these specimens is optimally performed when the specimens are freshly removed from the freezer

(Sanford et al., 2011). Each pinned specimen should carry its own label with both information specifics to entomological collection standards (Espeland et al., 2010) and case relevant information (Figure 6.11).

The management of these specimens after pinning and mounting requires particular attention to humidity levels and pest control. High humidity can

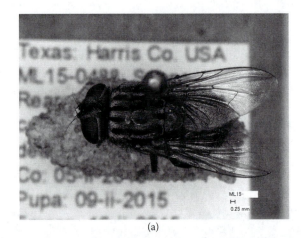

(a)

(b)

Figure 6.11 Reared adult flies are pinned using standard entomological procedures, to the right side of the midline through the thorax using entomological pins with their associated pupal case (if available). Each specimen is also labelled with standard entomological label information and case-relevant details.

cause specimens to become discoloured and to develop mould. Desiccants such as silica gel can be added to storage containers with pinned insects to avoid this in climates with high humidity. Pest control is another consideration when maintaining pinned insect specimens for an extended period of time. Even air-tight specimen storage boxes seem to become infested with pest insects such as carpet/hide beetles (Dermestidae) that can completely destroy pinned specimens. Standard moth balls with napthalene or paradichlorobenzene can be used to deter pest insects from feeding on pinned insect specimens. The suggested use of dichlorvos pest strips should be avoided as it has been found to impede DNA extraction from the specimens if any work is to be done with the specimens later (Tantawi and Greenberg, 1993).

Another exception is in specimen documentation and storage after collection and rearing. Larval flies are known to change over time during preservation even under optimal circumstances (Triplehorn and Johnson, 2005). Therefore, documentation of key features for species identification and larval length should be made in a reasonable timeframe after collection. Specimens should be stored so as to minimize preservative evaporation as this also alters specimens (Zehner et al., 2004). Using the preservation methods described above should preserve decedent DNA for later processing if required.

Similar to entomological museum collections, a management system for the specimens should be maintained in order to know when specimens have been shipped out and to whom they have been sent. Specimens may be sent to taxonomic experts or to other forensic entomologists for examination. Standard chain-of-custody forms with a courier that can provide documentation of delivery can be used for this purpose. One consideration that will be encountered when shipping is the consideration of shipping flammable ethanol. Some exceptions can be made for shipping small quantities of hazardous materials (DOT 173.4 and USPS Publication 52). Otherwise, specific training for packing and shipping hazardous materials will be required. Packaging of pinned specimens for shipping should include a hard inner package to prevent damage to the delicate insect specimens inside.

Mass Fatality

In many ways, management of multiple fatalities is an expansion of normal death scene operations. In fact, the characteristics of mass fatality incidents often enhance the importance of careful recovery methods. There may also be a concomitant shift in emphasis at both the scene and in the morgue from cause and manner of death (which may be evident in the circumstances of the incident) to decedent identification (which may be made more complex by body fragmentation and other taphonomic factors often associated with mass fatality incidents). There is also an inverse relationship between the complexity of an incident and the amount of contextual sources of prior

knowledge. A typical single decedent investigation involves an intact body
in an environment that provides significant prior knowledge to inform identification. For example, a person who dies in a car accident may have vehicle
registration bearing their name, photo identification in their pocket and be
accompanied by a surviving individual who can identify the decedent. As
the number of decedents and severity of trauma increases, so too does the
possibility that prior knowledge is lost and previous indicators of identification become complicated and/or non-existent; this is exacerbated with body
fragmentation.

As the level of incident complexity increases, the number of agencies
involved in the response typically increases as well. Clear communication
between agencies and pre-developed operational plans for the management
of decedents (fragmented or intact), evidence and property will aid in the
effective search, documentation and collection of these items during the
response. In most cases, the best approach to evidence management is a multidisciplinary team(s) of law enforcement (local, state and/or federal) and
medicolegal personnel at the incident site and in the morgue to reconcile
conflicting priorities in real time.

During the initial overall assessment of a mass fatality incident, agencies
involved in the scene response coordinate to determine the best evidence
management approach specific to that incident. Responders may elect to use
robust methods of evidence documentation, implementing tools such as total
station mapping, three-dimensional laser scanning or aerial photography to
specifically record the provenience of human remains, property and evidence
prior to recovery. In less complex incidents, responders may utilize simpler
methods of documentation such as hand-drawn maps using quadrants and
traditional photo documentation. Regardless of the documentation method
implemented, the chain-of-custody process generally follows the same principles employed for normal death scene operations: photo documentation,
written documentation and appropriate packaging.

Additional modifications may be made to the standard evidence management process to improve the efficiency of the overall investigation and
accuracy during a complex incident with a high volume of evidence. For
example, responding agencies may develop multiple incident site teams, with
each team responsible for one component of the evidence management process (e.g. search team, documentation team and recovery team). In the mass
fatality context, there are additional reasons for thorough documentation
and collection of evidence. Property items that may have been important
to inventory and collect for the family of the decedent during normal scene
investigations take on a new importance in the mass fatality context, particularly when typical indicators of a decedent's identity have been removed
by the circumstances of the incident. For example, on a scene with multiple
scattered and fragmented remains, a watch on the wrist of a severed arm

becomes a potential source of identification, and thus must be managed effectively.

Due to variable management of mass fatality incidents and associated evidence in the past, legislated transportation disasters, such as major aircraft accidents and rail passenger accidents, require specific response actions by the National Transportation Safety Board (NTSB) and responsible air or rail passenger carrier as dictated by Title 49 of the U.S. Code of Federal Regulations. This includes specific mandates for the management of evidence, primarily personal effects. The air carrier/rail passenger carrier must develop plans for the management of personal effects (which may include utilizing a third-party contractor) to be recovered, catalogued, cleaned to make safe and returned to the family. Any unclaimed personal effects must be retained for at least 18 months following the accident. Just as in all other incidents, the medicolegal authority maintains their authority over the human remains and associated personal effects (property found on the decedent), but may choose to transfer the personal effects to the same contractor managing unassociated personal effects (property found at the site but not on a decedent). For more information regarding the management of legislated transportation accidents, refer to the Federal Family Assistance Plan for Rail Passenger Disasters and the Federal Family Assistance Plan for Aviation Disasters developed by the NTSB.

Considerations and Conclusion

As with all theoretical best practices, the ideal strategy for management of medicolegal evidence is not always achievable. There are constraints that each medicolegal entity must contend with that have to do with resource availability, time limitations, logistics, funding, etc. In addition, identical evidentiary standards cannot be applied to all operations, but consistent management of different constraints is important. The medicolegal authority reconciles ideal operations with these constraints on a daily basis. The same standards cannot be applied to all evidence. For example, it is typically a best practice not to leave evidence unattended and to package, label and seal items of evidentiary value between each use. This is often not practical in medicolegal death investigation. Analysis of human remains, particularly of a complete skeleton, may take multiple visits over an extended period of time and is dependent on careful arrangement of remains in anatomical order. In instances like these, best practice is to limit access to the evidence while it is unpackaged.

Proper evidence management in the medicolegal context has far-reaching consequences, aiding in the determination of cause and manner of death and decedent identification in single and multiple/mass fatality investigations.

Thorough documentation, both photographically and written, ensures maintenance of evidentiary chain of custody for the medicolegal authority and the law enforcement agencies investigating possible criminal activity.

References

Byrd, J. H., Lord, W. D., Wallace, J. R., and Tomberlin, J. K. (2010). Collection of entomological evidence during legal investigations. In J. H. Byrd and J. L. Castner (Eds.), *Forensic Entomology: The Utility of Arthropods in Legal Investigations* (pp. 127–175). Boca Raton, FL: CRC Press.

Espeland, M., Irestedt, M., Johanson, K. A., Akerlund, M., Bergh, J.-E., and Kallersjo, M. (2010). Dichlorvos exposure impedes extraction and amplification of DNA from insects in museum collections. *Frontiers in Zoology*, 7(1), 2. doi:10.1186/1742-9994-7-2

Sanford, M. R., Pechal, J. L., and Tomberlin, J. K. (2011). Rehydration of forensically important larval Diptera specimens. *Journal of Medical Entomology*, 48(1), 118–125.

Tantawi, T. I., and Greenberg, B. (1993). The effect of killing and preservative solutions on estimates of maggot age and forensic cases. *Journal of Forensic Sciences*, 38(3), 702–707.

Triplehorn, C. A., and Johnson, N. F. (2005). *Borror and Delong's Introduction to the Study of Insects* (7th ed.). Belmont, CA: Thompson Brooks/Cole.

Zehner, R., Amendt, J., and Krettek, R. (2004). STR typing of human DNA from fly larvae fed on decomposing bodies. *Journal of Forensic Sciences*, 49(2), 337–340. Retrieved from https://www.ncbi.nlm.nih.gov/pubmed/15027556

General Principles and Techniques of Trace Evidence Collection

7

PATRICK BUZZINI AND
JORN CHI-CHUNG YU

Contents

The Scope of Trace Evidence

Trace evidence is one type of physical evidence that is transferred or exchanged between objects, and it therefore provides a 'trace' as to the linkage for the objects or to the object's origin and as physical signs of activities. Oftentimes, this type of physical evidence is small in size and quantity, which explains why it is called trace evidence. Under this definition, almost anything can be trace evidence. In the evolution of modern forensic science, trace evidence has been classified as a subdiscipline of criminalistics that is concerned with the recognition, detection, collection, characterization, comparison and the interpretation of a variety of materials or patterns suspected to be associated with criminal activities. During the investigation stage of a case, the investigators are tasked to discover *material clues* in the field or at the laboratory in order to either facilitate the reconstruction of a case or produce investigative leads. The term *material clues* is suggested here to qualify traces (i.e. materials, morphological features and their spatial distribution) that have been recognized to bear potential informative value with respect to the case at hand as opposed to be mere physical entities (e.g. smears, particles, fragments, dried stains, etc.) present in a location. The goal of trace evidence collection is not just to identify a proper way to collect and preserve evidence for forensic analysis, but also to understand the way to identify material clues.

Trace evidence consists of any debris, fragments, particles, dried stains or volatile compounds from different types of mass-produced objects or naturally occurring substances that are often transferred in small amount and size, during a given activity of interest, and that bear demonstrative information for investigative and/or forensic purposes. Traces may be recovered in a variety of forms and sizes. According to a practical definition, trace evidence is any type of evidence that does not fall into a specific department/unit in a forensic laboratory. Typical examples of trace evidence are human and animal hair, textile fibres, ignitable liquid residues (ILRs), gunshot residue (GSR), surface coating (or paint), glass, cosmetics, soil and minerals, low explosives, tapes, lamp filaments, explosive residues, wood chips and botanical substances like pollen. It is not possible to provide a complete list to cover all materials, because each of them may carry different clues in each case scenario. However, from the perspective of crime scene investigation, the investigators should recognize that trace evidence covers both *materials and their spatial distribution* as clues for criminal investigation. Depending upon the physical, chemical or biological characteristics of different types of traces, investigators can utilize trace evidence as the physical evidence with which to associate or discriminate suspects, objects and crime scenes during the investigation of a specific case.

As mentioned above, the notion of *variety* applies to the different types of material clues, including sizes and forms. As a consequence, a variety of methods and procedures for their collection are available to crime scene investigators and laboratory examiners. The generation of any type of traces during a particular activity and within a particular context occurs in an unplanned manner and under uncontrolled conditions. Therefore, traces can occur in varying quantity and quality, and very often constitute an imperfect record (De Forest, 2001).

It is common that the investigators may focus their search on the detection of physical evidence types that lead to the identity of individuals (e.g. biological fluids residue that leads to DNA analysis, visualization of latent fingerprints for personal identification). In such cases, trace evidence may be neglected because it is not robust enough to address the question of 'who' or, more generally, the 'source attribution'. As a result, trace evidence is not the type of physical evidence that is routinely collected during crime scene investigations. It depends on the investigator's background, knowledge and experience in trace evidence. Therefore, different collection strategies of trace evidence may be carried out. If investigators fail to recognize the presence of material clues, no trace evidence will be collected at all. Currently, blood, hair, drug, firearms and fingerprints are among the routine types of physical evidence that are more frequently collected and examined in the forensic laboratory.

While the focus of forensic laboratories seems to be confined to testing operations and the delivery of reliable outcomes, the utility of trace evidence to a particular case depends on the entire process that trace evidence undergoes and on the uncertainties that arise in the course of that process. The potential of trace evidence is more explicit when dealing with the evaluation of the occurrences of *activities* and for the purpose of reconstructions. In most of the cases, factors that are related to what trace evidence should be collected are based on the investigator's experience and observation, types of crime under investigation and resources that the jurisdiction could provide. If the investigator fails to recognize the presence of material clues or to infer their presence in microscopic size, such materials and their spatial distribution will be neither documented nor collected. Whenever material clues are recognized, proper evidence collection and documentation are critical.

Approach to Trace Evidence Collection

Because the scope of trace evidence covers a wide range of material clues produced from either transfer or exchange between objects due to interactions, the collection of trace evidence can be very time consuming and challenging. During the investigation stage of a case, one of the purposes of collecting traces is to generate investigative leads. It is important to recognize and collect material clues as early as possible to prevent contamination. The collection of trace evidence is not merely based on the recognition of the presence of materials or patterns from a location. Instead, the investigator needs to evaluate which material or pattern is relevant to the case at hand. In other words, the investigators need to evaluate the context of the case in order to recognize material clues during the collection of trace evidence.

Two approaches may be adopted with regards to the collection of trace evidence: a targeted approach or a non-targeted approach. A targeted approach implies that the investigator has a working hypothesis in mind at the time of trace evidence collection. Information about the case is available and can prove helpful to make appropriate evaluations of relevancy for potential trace evidence. In this targeted approach of trace evidence collection, an operational strategy for the searching, collection and transportation of trace evidence is developed. The strategy usually involves a targeted search for traces and a collection process based on reasonable assumptions about the task at hand at the time of investigation. The collection of traces in the targeted approach aims to contribute to build the case. In this setting, it is important to keep in mind that, as stated by Kind (1987), hypotheses are temporary means that require continual testing against facts and against other possible hypotheses.

By contrast, in the non-targeted approach of trace evidence collection, the investigator does not have any working hypothesis at the time of trace evidence collection. Because 'anything can be trace evidence', a non-targeted approach is very similar to an inspection approach, such as house inspection, vehicle inspection, food inspection, health inspection, etc. The purpose of a non-targeted approach is to search for and collect visible or latent traces which might carry physical, chemical or biological characteristics (also referred to as attributes, signatures or features) in order to contribute to the case. The investigator may prepare a well-defined standard operating procedure (SOP) with a checklist for all possible materials and patterns having the potential to become clues or evidence. The investigators can follow the SOP to complete the assigned tasks during the investigation in a systematic, thorough fashion. Because only limited information is available at the time of the investigation, multiple objects are then collected from the scene and also obtained from persons of interest (i.e. suspects or victims). Search and selection of trace evidence is subsequently conducted at the laboratory. The non-targeted approach is more systematic and thorough; however, this approach has the potential to generate an overwhelming amount of physical evidence which could then consume the resources from any forensic laboratory.

It is the crime scene leader or manager's responsibility to ensure that material clues are recognized, documented and properly collected in the field or at the laboratory in each of the cases. During a crime scene investigation, some addition or damage of materials might be a clear indication of crime activity. For example, a broken window or a damaged door knob could be a reasonable clue of forced entry by perpetrators. In a non-targeted evidence collection approach, the damage pattern as well as any traces associated with the damage should be documented and collected for further laboratory examination. However, if the damage is caused by the law enforcement or family members in order to break into the scene to rescue victims, then that damage might become irrelevant to the investigation, because the material clues collected from the window or door knob will not assist in elucidation of the case. The association between the addition or removal of materials from a crime scene and the crime activity should be determined. Note that the investigators also need to evaluate any information collected during any time of the investigation. Be aware of any confirmation bias, and carefully adopt a proper collection approach for the task at hand. If there is no context at the time of evidence collection to identify material clues, a non-targeted collection approach is preferred.

Moreover, the strategy for search and collection of trace evidence may change depending on the progress of the investigation. The general practice for the recognition of physical evidence during crime scene investigation can be found from several textbooks (Lee et al., 2001; Fisher and Fisher, 2012; Gardner, 2011). Collection of trace evidence can be performed in the field or at the laboratory. In many cases, collection of material clues is executed by a mandated law enforcement agency. However, this does not preclude the probability of further trace evidence being discovered later and subsequently collected by consulting forensic scientists retained by either the prosecution or defence.

The general principles for trace evidence collection may be applied to special cases, for example, bioterrorist attacks, explosion, food poisoning, environmental pollution, wide animal protection, antique authentication, war crimes, etc. To deal with unique scenarios for such special cases as chemical warfare agents, nuclear materials, explosives, archaeological, pathological and anthropological materials, art work and novel controlled substances, collaboration between agencies with specialists of different backgrounds and expertise may be needed to form a special task force team for trace evidence collection.

In this chapter, we aim to describe the general principles and techniques for trace evidence collection.

General Principles for Trace Evidence Collection

Collection of Unknown Trace Materials in the Field

Material Clues Recognized in the Field

Some traces are visible to the naked eye because of their relatively larger size and sufficient contrast against the surface where they are deposited. They can occur in various forms such as transferred marks, particles, debris, fragments, stains or dried stains, imprints, etc. Common examples are

- Coloured paint smears on vehicle bumpers
- Tufts of textile fibres on grids or broken windows at properties

- Hairs in a trunk or on a windshield of a vehicle
- Surface alteration of a wall with deposition of lead residues and removal of drywall and paint following an impact with a bullet
- Stains of a suspected toxic substance

Figure 7.1 shows a typical example of visible paint smear as a trace in a hit-and-run case. A magnifying glass may assist with visualization. These traces need first to be recognized, documented and then collected by the investigators. Their prospective connection to the case at hand must be assessed. This requires a judgement of the relevancy of the observed traces to the case. Collection is then preceded by documentation. De Forest (2005) distinguishes between passive and active documentation. Passive documentation includes the documentation of the state of the scene and its details prior to recognizing relevant traces. Active documentation involves the documentation of material clues.

Objects Recovered in the Field Suspected to Bear Traces

In many instances, trace evidence is not immediately recognized at the scene, especially when it occurs in microscopic forms. In these situations, crime scene investigators need to adopt a *microscopical approach*. In order to detect trace evidence, one must ask an important question: 'If a given activity did occur under particular circumstances and a particular location, which traces would be expected to be transferred and having persisted?' Developing such questions is probably the hardest intellectual exercise that an investigator

Figure 7.1 Typical transfer and exchange of material clues in a hit-and-run case.

is confronted with. Information about the context of the case is necessary to frame the most relevant questions, and at the same time, the investigator needs to consider alternative scenarios to prevent tunnelling the investigation. Based on this type of reasoning, objects are collected at the scene and brought to the laboratory for microscopical inspection and/or chemical extractions. Nickolls (1956) described a classic example of a burglary case where the crime scene investigator submitted broken glass to the laboratory after anticipating the presence of fibres, although he did not recognize them himself. The basis of this submission was that the investigator hypothesized that *the intruder must have come into contact with the glass and should have left traces of himself behind.*

The response is to collect any type of relevant objects that could be safely transported to the laboratory for further inspection of minute materials or microscopic features. The preservation of any trace evidence potentially deposited on seized items is thereby ensured during this process. Other examples include bed sheets, garments, shoes and weapons of all kinds.

Surfaces at Crime Scenes Suspected to Bear Traces

This applies to instances in which the recovery of traces is anticipated on surfaces or large objects that are not transportable to the laboratory. Examples include outdoor public surfaces, walls, window frames and large furniture. The same reasoning as in the previous point is applicable. The response would be to apply collection methods in situ. The use of a magnifying glass and alternate light sources may help detect particles of interest. Some examples include:

- Debris of burnt wooden floor suspected to carry impregnated ILRs
- Carpet areas searched using an electrostatic lifting apparatus (ESLA) for the detection of dusted footwear impressions
- GSRs around suspected bullet impact points

Collection of Unknown Trace Materials at the Laboratory

The laboratory should offer all types of supplies and equipment dedicated to the collection of trace evidence. A contamination-free area that accommodates the inspection of seized objects of varying size is crucial. A stereomicroscope is necessary for the inspection of the seized objects. A large surface table equipped with a surgical stereomicroscope offers the ideal conditions. Alternate light sources are also helpful in some instances. The context of the case dictates the types of traces that need to be collected. A *from general to particular* approach is employed. Objects believed to carry microscopic traces are first observed by the naked eye and followed by a close-up observation using a stereomicroscope with magnifications ranging from 10× to 100×. Different methods of collection are applied as described in the 'Collection of Unknown Trace Materials from Persons of Interest' section. Every step must be properly documented. If at all possible, it is important to document the location and the quantity of the recovered particles on a given object. This can be important during the phase of evidence interpretation when the question about the modalities of the occurrence of a given activity needs to be addressed. In most cases, the location of the recovered particles cannot be reliably ascertained due to poor collection practices (e.g. crumpled up garments). The container used for the transportation of the seized items must also be searched for loose particles.

Collection of Unknown Trace Materials from Persons of Interest (Suspects or Victims)

While objects belonging to persons of interest, such as garments, shoes or various accessories, can be seized and searched at the laboratory as described in the 'Techniques for Trace Evidence Collection' section, potential trace evidence may have been transferred and persisted on individuals themselves. Areas such as skin and hair are typical surfaces requiring inspection. Obviously, hands may be very informative since they are integrally used the most to perform all types of activities. Locard (1948) the importance of searching fingernails since they may retain particles resulting from the most recent occupations and activities of a suspect. If the presence of an individual in a given environment needs to be evaluated, the search of other parts such as nostrils or ear channels can provide useful results. Icard's work on dust in ears demonstrated the fact that every person who has been in a dusty place for any length of time retains the token of that place in the external auditory canals of his ears (Icard, 1921). Consideration of the type of case and its context may suggest body areas required to recover pertinent traces.

Collection of Known Origin Materials from Persons or Objects of Interest

Laboratory forensic examinations are often comparative in nature, i.e. comparisons between questioned traces and known materials. Various types of microscopical examinations and chemical analyses (mainly instrumental) are applied to characterize recovered specimens and to compare them to materials of known origin. The question about a common source is often of interest. Materials of known origin need to be properly obtained from persons (i.e. suspects or victims) or from objects of interest (i.e. items seized from suspects or victims). These are also known as reference samples. Usually, reference samples are in pristine condition and in abundant quantities compared to the unknown or questioned traces. Reference samples normally constitute a portion of the seized items. The scientist conducts an informed selection of what she is going to collect and analyze. The sampling process is intended to obtain a representative portion of the entire seized item. Examples include the collection of:

- Reference hairs from different areas of the head of an individual
- Reference fibres from two or more sets of interlaced yarns of a woven textile fabric
- Inked impressions of shoes seized from a suspect
- A roll of tape believed to be used to assemble an improvised explosive device (IED)
- A fingernail of a victim in order to attempt a physical match with a nail fragment recovered from the garments of an assault suspect

When applicable, another important practice is to collect a sample of the surface bearing the material clues to verify that there is no interference from the substrate. This is referred to as a comparison sample. Figure 7.2 shows an example of paint smears on the blade of a crowbar.

Collection of Known Origin Materials in the Field

The collection of known origin materials can be directly carried out in the field, i.e. at crime scenes or traffic accident scenes, if it is judged unnecessary or unfeasible to transport objects to the laboratory. Representative sampling applies to this instance as well. Examples include the collection of:

- Soil samples or botanical samples from different areas where a person of interest is suspected to have been
- Paint samples from a forced door at a burglarized property or from a damaged vehicle
- Large fragments of a broken window

In some cases, collection following an informed selection goes beyond representative sampling. For example, the goal of sampling adequate paint samples from a vehicle is not necessarily to represent the paint system of the entire vehicle. Areas that are undamaged are not relevant and, more importantly, are likely to exhibit different microscopical and chemical

Figure 7.2 Seized crowbar carrying transferred red paint smears. The surface of this tool is covered with a black paint. When isolation of the red smear cannot be carried out with the guarantee of not collecting the paint from the tool, the tool paint needs to be collected as a comparison sample and analyzed with the same methods (i.e. infrared spectroscopy) to verify that the tool paint does not interfere in the signal of the unknown specimen (i.e. red smear).

characteristics than those directly adjacent to the damaged areas. In this particular instance, paint samples must be collected near the damaged areas to ensure the proper conditions for conducting adequate comparative examinations.

Comparison samples must also be collected from the surrounding areas of the environment where unknown trace materials have been detected or are anticipated to be present. Examples include:

- Sampling for GSR in areas away from the location where the shooting has occurred to verify whether or not that particular environment is exposed to GSR on a regular basis or for reasons not related to the alleged incident
- Sampling for ILRs in an area of the floor nearby a suspected area of origin of a fire to verify if ILRs are normally part of that environment

Techniques for Trace Evidence Collection

Various methods and techniques are available to collect trace evidence. Some are specific to certain types of trace materials, whereas others are more versatile. The same materials can occur as traces exhibiting different forms and therefore the selected collection methods should cope with this aspect as well. For example, glass fragments can be recovered in large numbers and sizes at accident scenes, or in millimetric sizes on the garments of an individual suspected of having smashed a window; glass particles can also occur in powder form on a bullet having impacted through a window. Paint can be recovered in the form of multilayered fragments, in the form of abrasions or in the form of droplets if produced by a spray can. Textiles can be recovered as individual fibres, but also in the form of yarns (e.g. cordage), or in the form of torn pieces of fabric. Different packaging containers are also used for the storage and transportation of items of evidence. Preservation of evidence is a key factor to ensure the integrity of the evidence and to avoid degradation or contamination of the properties that will be studied analytically. One of the important concepts in trace evidence collection is that the investigator should have a general understanding of the physical, chemical or biological signatures that are associated with the searched traces. From the investigative point of view, it is critical that the collection method be tailored appropriately for the laboratory analysis. Ideally, when collecting trace evidence, the investigator needs to understand the back-end analytical protocols for the specific traces collected in the field. When in doubt, the investigator should always consult with the trace evidence specialist before formulating the collection strategy.

Hand Picking

Hand picking follows recognition of material clues in the field or on various items brought to the laboratory. Large objects are stored in appropriate containers to ensure the preservation of potential microscopic traces. Smaller size objects or material clues can be picked using fine-tip forceps or tweezers.

This method allows for documenting the exact location of collection and the number of particles that are collected. This information may prove useful for addressing questions related to alleged activities or for purposes of crime scene reconstruction.

Hand picking is a method of choice at the laboratory as well. Seized items, such as garments, sheets, shoes or weapons, are first inspected visually by the naked eye, followed by a search ultilizing a stereomicroscope. The recovery of particles is documented and the appropriate tool is used to isolate and secure them in an appropriate container. Particles too minute to be picked using tweezers can be collected using a needle. It is convenient to hold the needle at a low grazing angle (<15°) with respect to the surface where the particles of interest lie (Teetsov, 1977). Tungsten needles are very efficient for conducting micromanipulations. They can be obtained by heating the tip of a tungsten wire in contact with sodium nitrate. This process produces an exothermic reaction to form sodium tungstate. The result will be a fine-tipped needle (Delly and McCrone, 1973). A needle can be used successfully to scratch microscopic portions of smears and dried stains adhered to a given surface. The needle tip can be tucked delicately into the surface of the smear at a grazing angle and then be rolled so that the surface material can be peeled off the smear. This sort of micromanipulation needs to be conducted using a stereomicroscope. Both incident and transmitted light are helpful to visualize different sorts of traces under the microscopic scale.

Scraping

Scraping is meant here in a general sense and refers to the removal of particles from a given surface by applying some kind of friction. Scraping can be achieved on large to minute surfaces. However, the appropriate tools have to be selected for this type of collection method. Their choice depends on the types of materials to be collected, their size, their quantity and the nature and potential interference of the surface carrying them. Palenik and Palenik (2005) described the use of a metal spatula to scrape down clothing, especially if relatively large debris such as hairs or long fibres are targeted. They indicate the inefficiency of this method to recover microscopic size particles as well as the high potential of contamination (and the limited control over it) with particles in the surrounding environment.

On a smaller scale, when traces typically occur in the form of smears or dried stains, it is advisable to delicately scrape them using a sharp razor blade or a scalpel. The former is generally more efficient than the latter, because razor blades are more stable and precise. If this operation needs to be carried out on a vertical surface (e.g. a vehicle involved in a road accident or lead residue of a bullet after impact with a wall), it is highly recommended to place a piece of paper underneath the scraped area to avoid the loss of particles falling due to gravity. Particles almost certainly stick to the blade after its application and therefore it is a good practice to transmit the razor blade or scalpel to the laboratory in order to isolate the particles of interest with a needle under a stereomicroscope.

This method, however, involves high risks to collect material from the substrate where the smear is deposited. A comparison sample must be collected from a nearby area as described in the 'Collection of Known Origin Materials from Persons or Objects of Interest' section. Fingernails are generally apposite shells that offer a high potential for preservation of trace evidence. Debris can be recuperated by gently applying a rounded or flat end of a wooden toothpick. A different toothpick needs to be used for each finger, whereas an unused toothpick can be collected separately as a blank. Fingernails can also be cut using a clean nail clipper and the cuttings sealed separately in appropriate containers such as paper bags.

Combing

Combing is typically carried out on hairy surfaces of humans and animals in order to obtain reference samples. It is a method that allows collecting multiple hairs from a given area in a short amount of time. This method is also generally efficient to pick a representative sample of the hairy area of interest since multiple hairs are detached simultaneously. Also, combing proves useful in cases where hairy surfaces bear some sorts of particles. In the case of hairs, they will serve as piggybacks for smaller particles that may inform, for example, about the exposure of an individual to a particular environment or a recent activity. In the specific case of hairs, plucking is also applied as part of the sampling process.

Swabbing

Another collection method that may be used by trace evidence examiners is the relatively straightforward swabbing technique (wet or dry). While cotton swabs are commonly utilized to collect stains of biological nature, this method can also prove advantageous to the trace evidence examiner. Swabbing consists of applying a device on a surface to remove a substance or particles of interest generally by adherence. Swabbing can be applied to wet or oily stains that cannot be recuperated with a pipette (e.g. transfer plastic pipettes) or other liquid containers. The use of a swab could also be exploited to collect any type of powders or smears of creamy appearance (e.g. cosmetics). In trace evidence, swabbing is typically applied to the collection of GSRs. Dedicated kits are available which can be applied directly to individuals' hands and face, such as the one shown in Figure 7.3. Swabbing can be applied analogously for the collection of explosive particles.

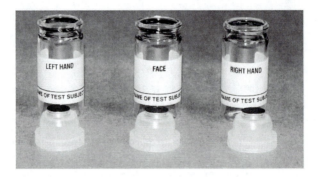

Figure 7.3 Example of collection kits for gunshot residues (GSRs). A kit consists of three adhesive stubs (i.e. sample holders) which are placed into contact with the three designated skin areas (left hand, face, and right hand), caps and transparent plastic containers. The kits are designed to accommodate the stubs so that they can be directly introduced in the sample chamber of the scanning electron microscope (SEM).

Tape Lifting

Tape lifting is a widely used collection method in the field. It is a classic method supposedly introduced in the forensic field by Swiss criminalist Frei-Sulzer (1951). A transparent adhesive tape of typical dimensions, approximately 5 cm wide and 20 cm long, is applied to a surface of interest to collect all sorts of particles and debris. The size of the tape can vary depending on the application. The tape can then be secured on a transparent acetate sheet to avoid loss and contamination. The size of the tape is chosen so that, of course, it does not exceed the size of the receiver acetate sheet. The adhesive tape can be applied more than once on a given surface. However, the operator has to avoid overpopulating the tape. Overcrowding the tape may result in difficulties to properly discern particles of interest during the microscopical search and also reduce the stickiness of the tape and subsequently its adherence to the acetate sheet. After tape lifting, the tapes are then examined for material clues at the laboratory using a stereomicroscope. The tape is systematically searched and the particles are counted and grouped. Placing a white paper with a grid under the transparent tape and acetate sheet can facilitate documentation of this detection process as the grid has numbers and letters to track each one of its squares. An extra transparent acetate sheet can be placed over the tape where permanent markers of various colours can be used to map the presence of the detected particles. This step is often time consuming especially if a high rate of other particles consisting of background noise are present. Alternate light sources or a fluorescence stereomicroscope may reveal fluorescent properties of some of the particles present on the tape.

Next, the particles of interest need to be extracted for further examinations. An incision with a scalpel is made around the particle and a droplet of an appropriate solvent (e.g. xylene) is applied to dissolve the adhesive component of the tape. The particles can now be transferred easily with forceps or a needle. Tape lifting is the method of choice for collecting single textile fibres suspected of having been transferred to a given surface. Chable et al. (1994) have tested a fully soluble tape for the recovery of fibres. De Wael et al. (2008) have tested the efficiency of five different adhesive tapes to collect fibre evidence. In addition to applying the method described above, the possibility exists to apply tapes on large surfaces such as a dead body in a serial, organized and numbered manner so that the distribution of the fibres on such surfaces is preserved. This is known as 1:1 taping (Springer, 1999).

The potential interference of the tape components during chemical analyses may be a source of concern. Traces isolated from lifted tapes may carry some residue of the tape (i.e. adhesive part). It is good practice to carefully observe the isolated traces under the stereomicroscope and wash them, for example, with ethanol. Although the risk of interference is low, it is advisable to analyze the tape components themselves. In the case of paint, Bernhard (2000) has verified that no interference occurred in spectra obtained with Fourier transform infrared (FTIR) spectroscopy and microspectrophotometry (MSP).

Vacuuming

In the collection process of physical evidence, it is occasionally necessary to inspect and sample a relatively large area in the field or a large surface like clothing. The vacuuming method is extremely beneficial for this purpose. This method is particularly helpful if the priority is to process a scene or items of evidence within a very short period of time. Furthermore, vacuuming allows for the collection of particles that are embedded in a surface (i.e. garments) too. It can be used to collect particles of size larger than 1 mm, like glass fragments or finer animal hairs, as well as microscopic particles, such as pollen, paint chips or foodstuffs particulates. Söderman and O'Connell (1952) in Europe and Kirk (1949) in the United States have described the vacuuming method and its uses to collect traces of forensic interest.

In order to collect particles, a regular vacuum hose is equipped with an air filter cassette. In certain models the filter device is placed behind a wand. The cassette is equipped with a clear methacrylate plastic that allows fine particles to pass through. On the top of the cassette is a piece of filter paper used to retain the particles of interest from passing through. The cassette or the wand is systematically applied over the surface to be searched. It can be used on the ground, on areas such as points of entry at crime scenes, on

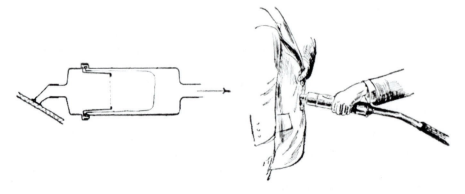

Figure 7.4 Illustration of the vacuuming system developed by Söderman and Heuberger. The filter to be attached to the vacuum cleaner (left) is applied on the garments directly by an individual (right). (From Söderman, H. and O'Connell, J. J., *Modern Criminal Investigation*, Funk & Wagnalls, New York, 1952.)

seized objects such as clothing or shoes, inside vehicles or on individuals themselves, for example, when they are temporarily detained. For garments, areas such as pockets and cuffs should be searched. The early Söderman model is shown in Figure 7.4.

After vacuuming, the filter paper is removed from the apparatus and can be transferred into a petri dish so that the contents can be observed, sorted and isolated under a stereomicroscope. Microscopic particles may need to be mounted microscopically for their inspection and sorting. The paper filter should be carefully wrapped in a smooth sheet, such as photographic paper. The photographic paper can be folded in order to obtain a funnel shape. The funnel is then oriented towards a microscopy glass slide. A tuning fork can be placed into contact with the paper in order to generate vibrations and induce the particles to fall down onto the slide.

An inconvenience of the vacuuming method is that there is a high potential for collecting irrelevant debris. If the method itself is fast, the sorting process may not be. This issue should be taken into consideration before using the vacuuming method, especially if the particles of interest risk are being mixed with a large amount of background noise, leading to the contamination of materials.

Batting or Shaking

Recuperating particles fallen by gravity is a simple and straightforward approach. The challenge is to secure a contamination-free environment where the particles will land. Two methods are discussed here, batting and shaking, both of which are primarily applied to garments. In batting, garments are hung over a table with a large surface, which is equipped with a clean white paper. A cloth beater is used to hit the garment and induce the particles to fall. Particles of relatively large size are then collected with forceps. Oblique lighting allows for visualization and facilitates the collection process. This method is not appropriate, however, if the particles of interest are of microscopic size (i.e. dust, minerals, botanical debris). An extra step would be required to recuperate them from the receiving surface. However, batting can be carried out after the object of interest (i.e. a garment) is wrapped into a sealed container. For instance, (Gross, 1893) described a case where a coat was seized at a crime scene. The coat was placed in a well-gummed paper bag that was vigorously beaten with sticks. Dust particles were then recovered and identified as wood, gelatin and powdered glue.

Shaking follows the same procedure as batting. The main difference is that a person holds the garment and then vigorously shakes it. Shaking is also one of the methods used to recover glass fragments (Hamer, 2001).

Criteria for Adopting Collection Methods for Trace Evidence

It has already been emphasized that different methods of collection are available to cope with the variety of materials that constitute the realm of trace evidence. These methods are adapted to the variety of forms in which traces can occur. Collection methods are also suitable to the potential poor quality, minute size and small amounts resulting from the nature of their transfer as well as their persistence on a given surface.

Collection methods are also selected for their efficiency. In this context, the concept of efficiency refers to the ability of a method to collect the highest number or quantity of debris of interest with regards to the total number of such debris on a given surface. In a quantitative way, it is the ratio between the number or quantity of recovered debris divided by the total number of debris that have been transferred and that have persisted on a given surface, excluding those that constitute background noise. Clearly, it would be difficult and time consuming to implement comprehensive studies to explore this criterion. The efficiency of a method could be evaluated in a relative manner while comparing several methods between them. For example, Ruffell et al. showed the superior performance of ultrasonic agitation for soil resulting in the recovery of more than 300 grains from socks compared to roughly 50 grains collected by means of brushing (Ruffell and Sandiford, 2011).

It is also possible to apply more than one collection method in sequence in order to maximize collection efficiency. The approach ranges from the least invasive to the most invasive method and from the most selective (described below) to the least selective method. For example, for recovering glass fragments on garments a visual search is typically followed by shaking. Fragments greater than 1.0 mm are more easily recovered by a visual search rather than those smaller than 1.0 mm. The possibility of those traces being overlooked will increase with the decrease of their size. The shaking method offers the highest potential to recover more fragments hidden in the structure of the fabric. So, then, why is shaking not used at the beginning? The answer is selectivity.

Selectivity refers to the attribute of a method to locate a particle of interest on a given surface and to collect it without removing any other surrounding particles that consist of interference or background noise. The definition of selectivity by the International Union of Pure and Applied Chemistry (IUPAC) for chemical analyses applies here. Selectivity refers to the extent to which the method can be used to determine particular analytes in mixtures or matrices without interference from other components of similar behaviour (International Union of Pure and Applied Chemistry, 2001). In forensic practice, if the investigated environment (e.g. a crime scene) has not been disturbed and if collected objects (i.e. garments) have been properly packaged for later inspection at the laboratory, the location, number or quantity, the dimensions and the form of the detected traces can be properly documented. This information may prove extremely useful to help investigators corroborate suspects' or victims' statements about the occurrence of an incident, confirm and qualify the nature of a supposed contact or establish a sequence of events.

Another important expectation from any selected collection method is the guarantee of permanent preservation. It may be difficult to maintain the control over traces especially in the form of microscopic particles. It is also highly advisable to manipulate seized items at a minimum, especially for fragile traces. This means that a given collection method shall favour the passage from a recovery step to an analytical step with a minimum amount of intervention on the part of laboratory personnel. Excellent examples are the methods for collection of GSR and ILRs from fire debris. The systems that have been developed for these two types of substances, for example, can be straightforwardly introduced in a dedicated instrument. In the context of fire debris analysis, it is common to hang a strip of activated charcoal inside the metal can used to collect debris thought to be impregnated with ignitable liquids. In the headspace of the debris, the strip adsorbs potential ILRs. The strip is then introduced in an insert and in a vial (with a polypropylene cap for autosampling by the instrument) along with a solvent to complete the extraction process by desorption. The vial is then introduced in the autosampling injecting device of the gas chromatograph/mass spectrometer (GC-MS) ready for analysis (Newman et al., 1996; Stauffer et al., 2008). This process is shown in Figure 7.5.

GSRs are typically transferred on a round adhesive surface (usually carbon) of a stub. After verifying the presence of potential contaminants using a stereomicroscope, the stub is directly introduced in the sample holder of the scanning electron microscope (SEM) for the morphological study of the residues and their elemental analysis. This process is shown in Figure 7.6.

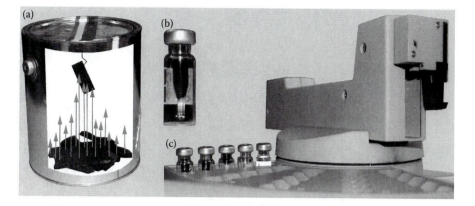

Figure 7.5 Introduction in a gas chromatogram/mass spectrometer (GC-MS) of suspected ignitable liquid residue (ILR) from fire debris collected in a paint can. (a) A strip of activated charcoal is suspended inside the metal can where it is exposed to the headspace of the debris: the strip adsorbs ILRs, if present. (b) The strip is introduced in an insert inside a vial with a solvent. (c) The vial is then introduced in the autosampling injecting device of the GC-MS.

Figure 7.6 Close-up view of the sample chamber of the SEM. The arrow indicates the stub carrying potential GSR which is directly places into the sample holder.

Finally, practical aspects such as rapidity and simplicity of application are also considered when looking to adopt a given collection method. Usually, rapid methods for collection are those more susceptible to collect irrelevant particles present as background noise. The time saved in the field may need to be recuperated at the laboratory where selection and sorting will be conducted with a stereomicroscope. Figure 7.7 features the relationship between selectivity and rapidity for a number of commonly used collection methods.

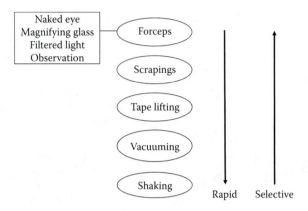

Figure 7.7 Relationship between the factors of selectivity and rapidity that qualify the methods that are commonly used for the collection of unknown specimens in the field or at the laboratory.

Note that the least selective collection techniques, although swift, will result in the loss of information about the exact location where microscopic traces are collected.

Quality Assurance Considerations

There are several guidelines for trace evidence handling and collection established at both the state and federal levels. The former Scientific Working Group on Materials Analysis (SWGMAT) published 'Trace Evidence Recovery Guidelines' in 1999. The *Handbook of Forensic Services* published by the Federal Bureau of Investigation (FBI) provided information to facilitate the field-laboratory collaboration for a successful collection of traces (United States Department of Justice, Federal Bureau of Investigation, 2013). Many states also produced similar handbooks to assist the field investigator to collect traces, including Texas and Virginia. Texas, Virginia, etc. The ASTM E1188-11 – Standard Practice for Collection and Preservation of Information and Physical Items by a Technical Investigator Standard (American Society for Testing and Materials, 2017) provided the requirements and guidelines for the collection and preservation of information and physical items by any technical investigator pertaining to an incident that can be reasonably expected to be the subject of litigation. Some forensic laboratory systems have developed field kits for trace evidence collection and preservation. Common tools, such as scalpels, tweezers, zip-lock plastic bags, round metal 'pill-boxes', paper envelopes and evidence seals have been included within those kits to assist with the collection of traces. In the trace laboratory, the stereo-microscope is the most useful tool to discover and examine trace evidence.

In the future, SOPs, inspection checklist models or project management models may be established for both targeted and non-targeted collection approaches in order to ensure the quality of trace evidence collection. The problem of contamination has been addressed by implementing measures to an environment where crime scene investigators and laboratory personnel respectively adopt approaches that are as least invasive as possible. Personal protective equipment including gloves, masks and foot covers are routinely used to avoid contamination. Laboratory facilities can be organized to separate rooms dedicated to the search of unknown specimens and samples of known origin respectively. Inspection of questioned and reference items can also occur on different days. Laboratory cleaning times can be monitored and tracked. All work should be documented in detail by means of laboratory notes. Nowadays, trace evidence examinations, including the critical step of collection, are expected to follow validated and transparent, documented contamination-free protocols and practice.

Summary

This chapter emphasized the importance of properly collecting trace evidence in the field and at the laboratory. Since the 1970s, most societies have developed an awareness to recognize that the solution of major crimes will hinge upon the discovery of physical evidence at crime scenes and its subsequent scientific laboratory analysis (Peterson and Anna, 2006). Impartial and objective results, which are relevant, accurate, with known uncertainties, are highly expected from all levels of forensic science. Criminal investigation is the duty of a criminal justice system in a society. Under limited resources and funds, forensic laboratories from different jurisdictions have reduced their operations related to trace evidence examination. Also, the DNA model has impacted on the reporting of trace evidence. Because anything present at the scene could be material clues and could become valuable trace evidence to address forensic questions, it is important to understand both the targeted and non-targeted approaches. The strategies to search, detect and collect traces are consequent. Different collection methods can be utilized to successfully secure the preservation of various types of debris that can be recognized as contributing to a case. The variety of the materials that constitute the realm of trace evidence and the variety of the forms that they assume after their separation from an originating entity both explain the variety of methods that have been devised to collect prospective trace evidence.

The collection step not only requires rigour in terms of properly choosing and using a given method (or a sequence of methods) and the appropriate containers. This important process encompasses an anticipated understanding of the contribution of collected specimens and collected reference samples from the part of the crime scene investigator and/or the forensic scientist. Information such as the location and quantity of traces recovered at a crime scene or on an item inspected at the laboratory shall be recorded as reliably as possible because it allows for valuing the highest contribution of trace evidence: addressing questions about the occurrences of claimed activities and about reconstructive aspects.

References

American Society for Testing and Materials (ASTM E1188-11). (2017). Standard Practice for Collection and Preservation of Information and Physical Items by a Technical Investigator. West Conshohocken, PA: ASTM International. www.astm.org.

Bernhard, W. (2000). Paint and tape: Collection and storage of microtraces of paint in adhesive tape. *Journal of Forensic Sciences*, 45(6), 1312–1315.

Chable, J., Roux, C., and Lennard, C. (1994). Collection of fiber evidence using water-soluble cellophane tape. *Journal of Forensic Sciences*, 39(6), 1520–1527.

De Forest, P. (2005). Crime scene investigation. *Encyclopedia of Law Enforcement*, 1, 111–116.

De Forest, P. R. (2001). What is trace evidence? In B. Caddy (Ed.), *Forensic Examination of Glass and Paint—Analysis and Interpretation* (chap. 1, pp. 1–25). London, Philadelphia: Taylor & Francis.

De Wael, K., Gason, F. G. C. S. C., and Baes, C. A. V. (2008). Selection of an adhesive tape suitable for forensic fiber sampling. *Journal of Forensic Sciences*, 53(1), 168–171.

Delly, G., and McCrone, W. (1973). *The Particle Atlas* (Vol. 1, 2nd ed.). Ann Arbor, MI: Ann Arbor Publishing.

Fisher, B., and Fisher, D. (2012). *Techniques of Crime Scene Investigation*. Boca Raton, FL: CRC Press.

Frei-Sulzer, M. (1951). Die Sicherung von Mikrospuren mit Klebeband. *Kriminalistik*, 10, 190–194.

Gardner, R. M. (2011). *Practical Crime Scene Processing and Investigation*. Boca Raton, FL: CRC Press.

Gross, H. (1893). *Handbuch für Untersuchungsrichter als System der Kriminalistik*. Munich: Schweitzer.

Hamer, P. (2001). Microscopic techniques for glass examination. In B. Caddy (Ed.), *Forensic Examination of Glass and Paint* (chap. 3, pp. 47–63). London: Taylor & Francis.

Icard, S. (June 1921). Le cérumen au point de vue médicolégal. *Annales d'Hygiène Publique et de Médecine Légale*, 4(35), 348–357.

International Union of Pure and Applied Chemistry. (2001). Selectivity in analytical chemistry. *Pure and Applied Chemistry*, 73(8), 1381–1386.

Kind, S. S. (1987). *The Scientific Investigation of Crime*. Harrogate: Forensic Science Services.

Kirk, P. L. (1949). Microscopic evidence-its use in the investigation of crime. *Journal of Criminal Law and Criminology*, 40(3), 362–369.

Lee, H. C., Palmbach, T., and Millerm, M. T. (2001). *Henry Lee's Crime Scene Handbook*. San Diego, CA: Elsevier Academic Press.

Locard, E. (1948). *Manuel de technique policière* (4th ed.). Paris: Payot.

Newman, R., Dietz, W., and Lothridge, K. (1996). The use of activated charcoal strips for fire debris extractions by passive diffusion. Part 1: The effects of time, temperature, strip size, and sample concentration. *Journal of Forensic Sciences*, 41(3), 361–370.

Nickolls, L. C. (1956). *The Scientific Investigation of Crime*. London: Butterworth & Co.

Palenik, S., and Palenik, C. (2005). Microscopy and microchemistry of physical evidence. In R. Saferstein (Ed.), *Forensic Science Handbook—Volume II* (2nd ed., chap. 5, pp. 175–230). Upper Saddle River, NJ: Pearson Prentice Hall.

Peterson, J. L., and Anna, S. L. (2006). The evolution of forensic science: Progress amid the pitfalls. *Stetson Law Review*, 36, 621.

Ruffell, A., and Sandiford, A. (2011). Maximizing trace soil evidence: An improved recovery method developed during investigation of a $26 million bank robbery. *Forensic Science International*, 209(1–3), E1–E7.

Scientific Working Group on Materials Analysis (SWGMAT). 1999. Trace evidence recovery guidelines. *Forensic Science Communications*, 1(3). Retrieved from https://archives.fbi.gov/archives/about-us/lab/forensic-science-communications/fsc/oct1999/trace.htm.

Söderman, H., and O'Connell, J. J. (1952). *Modern Criminal Investigation*. New York, NY: Funk & Wagnalls.

Springer, F. (1999). Collection of fibre evidence from crime scenes. In J. Robertson and M. Grieve (Eds.), *Forensic Examination of Fibres* (2nd ed., chap. 5.2, pp. 101–115). London: Taylor & Francis.

Stauffer, E., Dolan, J. A., and Newman, R. (2008). *Fire Debris Analysis*. Burlington, MA: Elsevier Academic Press.

Teetsov, A. S. (1977). Techniques of small particle manipulation. *Microscope*, 25, 103–113.

United States Department of Justice, Federal Bureau of Investigation. (2013). Handbook of Forensic Services. An FBI Laboratory Publication, Federal Bureau of Investigation, Quantico, Virginia. https://www.fbi.gov/file-repository/handbook-of-forensic-services-pdf.pdf. Accessed on April 21, 2017.

Firearms Evidence
Documentation, Collection and Preservation

8

JAY M STUART

Contents

Overall Approach

The collection and preservation of firearm-related evidence (firearms, fired ammunition components and unfired ammunition) should be documented using numerous photographs. Firearms specifically have a number of features that need to be taken into consideration and evaluated during the course of the investigation. Photographs, if taken correctly, of the scene and the evidence, will allow the investigator to answer numerous questions as the investigation progresses.

It is extremely beneficial to have scientifically minded investigators as a part of the crime scene team. These individuals will evaluate the evidence and possibly glean important information from it, instead of simply collecting the evidence. However, even more important is that the investigator needs to have basic training on what services the laboratory can and does provide. Without this knowledge, they could potentially alter or destroy what could be a crucial piece of evidence or fail to collect something due to this lack of understanding.

Indicator Systems

Over the past 12 years, this author has experienced a variety of different indicator systems. They range from simple number or letter designations to very complex alpha-numeric systems. The system that appears to work best is a simple alphanumeric, such as the following:

    a = Ammunition
    b = Blood
    c = Cartridge casing
    d = Document
    f = Firearm
    h = Hair
    i = Impact site
    k = Knife
    m = Miscellaneous
    n = Narcotic
    p = Projectile/fragment

The process of indicating evidence at a scene becomes very simple. If there are three projectiles recovered, they are designated p-1, p-2 and p-3. Just like a simple 1, 2, 3 system, this method does not in any way denote sequence of events, but rather it denotes the order in which items of evidence are noticed and marked.

There are multiple benefits of this system. First, while at the scene, the ability to visually differentiate the general types of evidence allows the investigator to discern any potential patterns, such as movement through the scene denoted by the cartridge-casing locations. Later in the investigation, when looking at photographs from the scene, the investigator can immediately identify what type of evidence he is looking at without needing to refer to a log that correlates a random number or letter to a piece of evidence.

This same concept also applies to scene diagrams. Homicide scene diagrams can get extremely confusing without any descriptive indicator systems (Figure 8.1). However, if the above indicator system is used, it is extremely easy to decipher what evidence is located where (Figure 8.2).

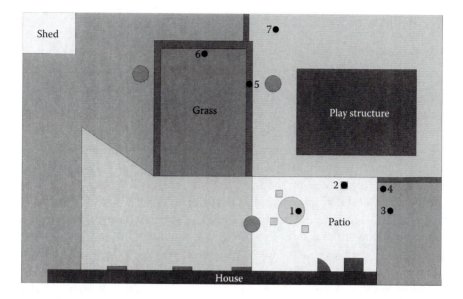

Figure 8.1 Scene diagram with numeric indicators. A person looking at this diagram would need a key to decipher which piece of evidence correlates with each number.

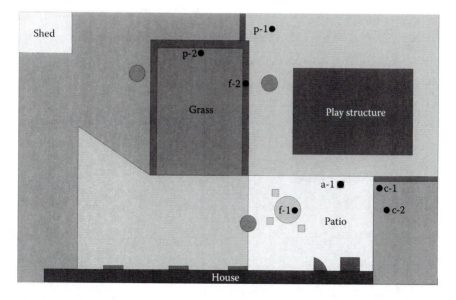

Figure 8.2 By using a simple alphanumeric system, a viewer can quickly determine which items are firearms, projectiles, cartridge casings and unfired ammunition.

Firearms

Photography

As with all evidence, the collection of a firearm should begin with a distant photograph showing the item's location within the overall scene (Figure 8.3). Follow that up with a mid-range photograph showing the item's relative location to another, ideally stationary, object in the scene. The next photo should be a close-up of the item, including an indicator, showing its precise location within the scene (Figure 8.4). The final photo in this initial group is an orthographic shot showing the firearm in the plane of the field of view with an indicator, and if appropriate, a scale visible (Figure 8.5).

The next set of four photographs, taken at a shallow angle, are of the front, back, top and bottom of the firearm to document its condition as it lies at the scene (Figure 8.6a through d). The best practice is for the investigator to move around the firearm. However, if scene conditions don't allow for this, the firearm can be rotated using a gloved hand. Once these photographs have been taken, the firearm should be flipped over, again with a gloved hand, keeping DNA and latent fingerprints in mind, and a photo of the opposite side taken (Figure 8.7).

Special attention should be given to photographically documenting any damage to the firearm, any malfunctions (Figure 8.8) and any visible trace evidence (Figure 8.9).

If the firearm is a semiautomatic, a good method of documenting the load condition is to take the cartridge out of the chamber (if present) and place it

Figure 8.3 Overall photo of the scene shows the location of the evidence within the scene.

Figure 8.4 Close-up of the firearm (with indicator).

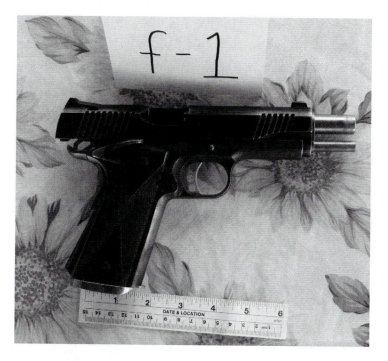

Figure 8.5 Orthographic photo of the firearm (with indicator and scale).

above the chamber. The cartridges from the magazine can be placed next to the emptied magazine, in the order in which they were removed, next to the firearm (Figure 8.10). It is also advisable to take a photo of the cartridge headstamps.

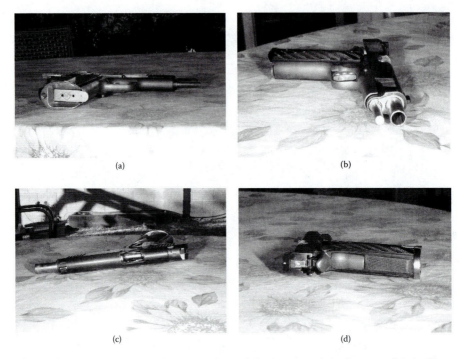

Figure 8.6 (a) Shallow angle photo taken of the bottom of the firearm. (b) Shallow angle photo taken of the front of the firearm. (c) Shallow angle photo taken of the top of the firearm. (d) Shallow angle photo taken of the back of the firearm.

Figure 8.7 Orthographic photo taken of the opposite side of the firearm.

Figure 8.8 Photograph showing the details of a malfunction.

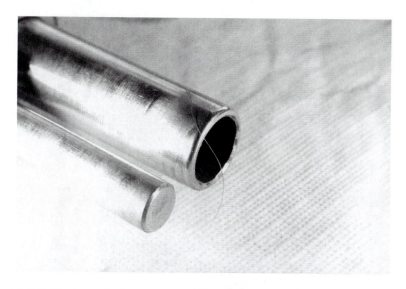

Figure 8.9 Photograph showing possible trace evidence (hair).

Depending on the type of firearm, additional photographs may need to be taken. If the firearm in question is a revolver, the cylinder should be scribed on both sides of the top strap using a permanent marker (Figure 8.11), allowing for the orientation of the cylinder at the time of exam to be documented. Once the cylinder is open, an overall shot of the cartridge case heads in relation to the top strap (Figure 8.12) should be taken. This image will nicely document the cartridge case locations, the relative headstamps and

Figure 8.10 Photograph showing the load condition of the firearm.

Figure 8.11 Photograph showing the top of the cylinder, scribed on either side of the top strap for orientation of the cylinder.

Figure 8.12 Photograph showing the headstamps of the fired and unfired ammunition in the cylinder.

Figure 8.13 Photograph showing the ammunition from the front of the cylinder as well as visible flares/halos around two of the chambers.

the presence or lack of firing pin impressions. A photo of the front of the cylinder will document any halos or flares (Figure 8.13).

These same basic principles can be applied to rifles and shotguns. The bottom line, especially in the digital age, is that you can never take too many photographs. If something doesn't look good in one of your photographs, be it lighting, clarity, etc., adjust your camera settings and take another photograph.

Collection and Preparation

When collecting firearms, there are a number of things to keep in mind. First and foremost is the possible collection of DNA and processing the evidence for latent fingerprints. The next is to think about what condition the firearm is in when it is recovered.

If the firearm is dry when it is recovered, then it can be packaged and tagged as evidence following the appropriate, lab-specific procedures. However, if the firearm is wet, either by mud, blood or water, other steps should be taken. If the firearm has a small amount of blood on the exterior surfaces, then it can typically be dried in a drying hood before tagging. If the firearm is saturated in blood or recovered in either water or mud, it is best to set up a time with the firearm unit in the laboratory to have the firearm disassembled, cleaned and treated with oil to prevent any rusting, while at the same time potentially collecting any necessary DNA or latent evidence if that is likely. For firearms recovered in mud/water, the best practice is to collect the firearm in a sample of the liquid it is in. For example, if the firearm is recovered from a local river, collect some of the river water (a five-gallon bucket works well) and place the firearm in it for transfer. The main point to keep in mind is not to allow the firearm to interact with the air. This begins the rusting process and can hinder any subsequent firearm examinations down the line.

Once the firearm is cleaned and dried, it can be tagged as evidence. The process for tagging evidence will differ from agency to agency, but the basic steps should be fairly consistent. The first step is to make the firearm safe. This means making sure that any unfired ammunition has been removed from the firearm/magazine and that the chamber is empty. Many agencies will want some sort of visual indication that the firearm is safe. A common practice is to put something in the action or barrel of the firearm to prevent it from firing, such as a zip tie or barrel plug. While this author is not a fan of putting anything down the barrel or action of a firearm, simply from a trace evidence standpoint, if this is the required method, use something made out of plastic, and at all costs, stay away from using metal.

Packaging

Again, packaging requirements will vary from agency to agency, but this author feels that the following method works well for packaging a firearm.

1. Once the firearm has been made safe, the firearm itself and any accompanying unloaded, magazine(s) should be placed in the required packaging material, whether that is a box or a plastic bag.
   a. Paper bags should never be used as the firearm will most likely tear through the bag.
   b. The reason for including the magazine(s) with the firearm is that it is becoming more common for firearm manufacturers to design their firearms with a magazine safety. This means that the firearm will not function without a magazine inserted. Having the magazine(s) with the firearm may help the firearm examiner during his examination.

2. Seal the package, including the date and initials of the person packaging the evidence.
3. Label the packaging with the appropriate information:
   a. Case number
   b. Item indicator (i.e. f-1)
   c. Collection location
   d. Collector's name
   e. Date of collection
   f. Time of collection

Projectiles

Photography

The procedure for photographing projectiles is similar to other evidence.
Start with an overall photograph (Figure 8.14) of the scene, with indicators,
showing the location of the projectile in the scene, followed by a mid-range
photograph (Figure 8.15) showing the item's location in relation to another
object in the scene. The final photograph (Figure 8.16) should be of the item
itself with an indicator and a scale.

At this point, the projectile can be collected, keeping in mind the preservation of any trace materials that might be present on the projectile. If the
crime scene investigator has the proper training, the projectile can be initially examined on scene. Different types of trace materials adhering to the
projectile can tell the investigator what object(s) the bullet impacted before

Figure 8.14 Overall photograph showing the location of the projectile.

Figure 8.15 Mid-range photograph showing the item's location in the scene.

Figure 8.16 Close-up of the projectile (with indicator and scale).

coming to rest. In addition, the types of damage observed on the bullet can assist the investigator *at the scene* in determining what impacted surfaces may require extra examination for impact sites.

Collection and Preparation

Once all of the necessary photographs have been taken, the projectiles can be collected. For the majority of them, it will be as simple as picking them up off the ground and placing them in the appropriate package. If the projectile has biological material adhering to it, it will need to be placed in a drying cabinet before packaging. If the projectile has to be collected from places such as a wall or from the door or seat of a vehicle, special care must be taken during the collection process. It is extremely important that metal tools not be used to collect a projectile from any material. The use of metal has the potential to mark or over-mark the important toolmarks on the bullet surface, hindering the work of the firearm examiner in the laboratory. If the projectile cannot be easily removed, then cut out a large section of the material and tag that as evidence. The firearm examiner can then take the necessary steps to remove the imbedded projectile.

Packaging

The ideal packaging of projectiles would be as follows:

1. Place each projectile in its own small package (paper or plastic bag or small box).
   a. Label each package with the item's indicator and collection location.
2. Seal the package, including the date and initials of the person packaging the evidence.
3. Place all of the smaller, individual packages into a single, larger package.
4. Label this larger package with the appropriate information:
   a. Case number
   b. Description of items contained within packaging (i.e. p-1 through p-6)
   c. Overall collection location
   d. Collector's name
   e. Date of collection
   f. Time of collection

5. Seal the larger package, including the date and initials of the person collecting the evidence.

Cartridge Casings

Photography

The photography of cartridge casings is the same as that for projectiles. Start with an overall photograph (Figure 8.17) of the scene, with indicators, showing the location of the casing in the scene followed by a mid-range photograph (Figure 8.18) showing the item's location in relation to another object in the scene. The final photograph (Figure 8.19) should be of the item itself with an indicator and scale.

Figure 8.17 Overall photograph showing the location of the cartridge casing.

Figure 8.18 Mid-range photograph showing the item's location in the scene.

Figure 8.19 Close-up of the cartridge casing (with indicator and scale).

At this point, the casing can be collected, keeping in mind the preservation of any trace materials that might be present.

Collection and Preparation

Collection of cartridge casings is fairly straightforward. Once all of the necessary photographs have been taken, the cartridge casings can be picked up and packaged. Care should be taken not to pick up the casings by placing any object in the casing mouth. Doing so has the potential to remove any trace material, such as paint transfer.

Packaging

The ideal packaging of cartridge casings would be as follows:

1. Place each casing in its own small package (paper or plastic bag).
   a. Label each package with the item's indicator and collection location.
2. Seal the package, including the date and initials of the person packaging the evidence.
3. Place all of the smaller, individual packages into a single, larger package.
4. Label this larger package with the appropriate information:
   a. Case number
   b. Description of items contained within packaging (i.e. c-1 through c-20)
   c. Overall collection location
   d. Collector's name
   e. Date of collection
   f. Time of collection
5. Seal the larger package, including the date and initials of the person collecting the evidence.

Ammunition

Photography

The collection of unfired ammunition is often done when a search warrant is served, although it can take place at the scene. While at the scene, the photography sequence is the same as with projectiles or cartridge casings: overall, mid-range and close-up with indicator. Following these photographs, it is appropriate to take photographs of the headstamps and if desired, the bullets as well. If there is a large amount of ammunition with the same headstamps and bullets, then a representative photo can be taken.

The investigator will most often come across boxed ammunition when a search warrant is served. Start by taking the standard overall, mid-range and close-up photographs. Once that is complete, take a photograph of all six sides of the ammunition box (Figure 8.20a and b). The investigator at this point can remove the ammunition from the box and take the appropriate photographs of the headstamps (Figure 8.21) and bullets (Figure 8.22).

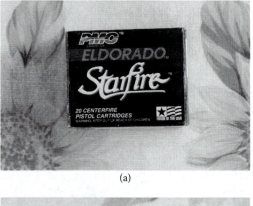

(a)

(b)

Figure 8.20 (a) Photograph of top of the ammunition box (this is one of six pictures taken of this ammunition package). (b) Photograph of one end of the ammunition box (this is one of six pictures taken of this ammunition package).

Collection and Preparation

Once the necessary photographs have been taken, then the evidence is ready to be collected. Take care to wear gloves when collecting boxes of ammunition. They can be a good source of latent prints.

Packaging

Like cartridge casings, ammunition is fairly straightforward when it comes to packaging. Making sure to document what the investigator is doing, it is helpful to tape closed the ammunition boxes. This would prevent the boxes

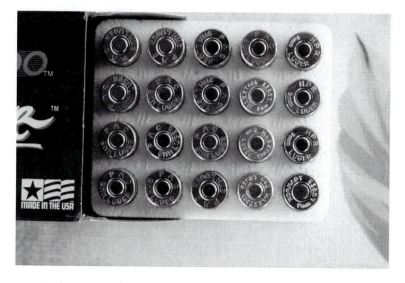

Figure 8.21 Photograph of all of the headstamps inside this ammunition box.

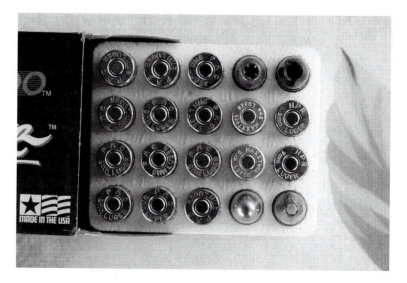

Figure 8.22 Photograph of a representative of each type of bullet contained within this ammunition box.

from opening up during transport/storage and the ammunition mixing together. The ideal packaging of ammunition would be as follows:

1. Place the boxes of unfired ammunition in a plastic bag (paper will tear).
   a. Ammunition collected from the same location (i.e. the closet) can be packaged in the same bag.

2. Seal the package, including the date and initials of the person packaging the evidence.
3. Label this package with the appropriate information:
   a. Case number
   b. Description of items contained within packaging (i.e. a-1)
   c. Collection location
   d. Collector's name
   e. Date of collection
   f. Time of collection

Introduction to Drug Evidence Handling Procedures

9

JASMINE DRAKE

Contents

Preventing the illicit manufacture and distribution of controlled substances and precursors is a global issue for law enforcement agencies. Illicit controlled substances or precursors are often encountered at crime scenes as physical evidence of drug production, trafficking and/or abuse. There are several special considerations, such as how to ensure secure transport and proper storage of evidentiary items and determining which safety precautions should be used in the collection of suspected controlled substances that must be addressed. The essential role of the forensic chemist is to analyse suspected drug evidence for the presence or absence of controlled substances. Forensic chemists also assist local and federal law enforcement agencies with evidence collection at crime scenes and clandestine laboratory investigations. In addition, they may serve as expert witnesses and provide testimony in court proceedings, when called upon.

Controlled substances are regulated by the Controlled Substances Act, which is a federal statute, that regulates the distribution, use and manufacture of controlled substances in the United States. In this legislation, controlled substances are categorized into five schedules based on (1) whether they have any accepted medical use for treatments in the United States, (2) their potential for abuse and (3) their likelihood of creating a drug dependence. For example, drugs like heroin and marijuana, which have no accepted medical use in the United States, a high potential for abuse and a high likelihood for dependence, can be found in Schedule I. In contrast, a drug such as cocaine, which has an accepted medical use in medical treatments in the United States as an anaesthetic, has a high potential for abuse and a high likelihood of dependence, is classified as a Schedule II controlled substance. On the other end of the spectrum, codeine (concentrations up to 200 mg/100 g), which has an accepted medical use, lower abuse potential and a lower likelihood of drug dependence, can be found in Schedule V. An annually updated list of the controlled substances and their schedules can be found in the Title 21 Code of Federal Regulations ([C.F.R.] §§ 1308.11 through 1308.15) (Schedules of Controlled Substances, 2015).

Scene Assessment and Documentation

Proper evidence collection, documentation and preservation of suspected drugs and precursors are integral parts of a forensic chemist's role at the crime scene. The forensic chemist's major role at the crime scene is to assist with proper evidence collection, prepare documentation and to make certain that precautions are taken in regards to chemical safety hazards, which may be present at the crime scene. The assessment of the possible safety hazards is an area of high importance, due to the various toxic gases, flammable solvents and volatile chemicals that are often encountered by crime scene personnel at clandestine laboratories, which are scenes where the illegal manufacture or synthesis of controlled substances takes place. As an initial step, a thorough evaluation of the crime scene, which should include a detailed discussion with the law enforcement officers present at the scene, should be conducted before any evidence is handled at the scene. At many scenes, the forensic chemist must coordinate efforts with other crime scene personnel or first responders present at the crime scene. For example, at a suspected methamphetamine clandestine laboratory, a latent print examiner may have to photograph and collect fingerprint evidence on vessels used for the illegal manufacture of the product, before the items can be handled by the forensic chemist. Before proceeding with collection of drug evidence, the forensic chemist should set up a clear strategic plan, which addresses the following considerations:

- Recognition of substances that should be collected
- Safety precautions and proper protective equipment (PPE) required to safely handle and collect evidentiary materials
- Types of equipment or collection tools that are suitable
- Systematic plan for photography, documentation and collection of the evidence items

Recognition of which items present at the crime scene are drug evidences is the next vital step in the process. Difficulty in the recognition of controlled substances, listed chemicals and precursor materials may be encountered by the crime scene examiner, since these evidentiary materials can be found in various forms, such as powders (visible and invisible), liquids, tablets, capsules, inhalants, injectable liquids, blotter paper and plant material. In addition, the forensic chemist or crime scene investigator will often encounter controlled substances or precursor materials at a crime scene that may be camouflaged or housed in different materials in an attempt to prevent detection. In these cases, it is essential that the analyst uses the scientific method and makes very careful observations at the crime scene. For example, at a clandestine laboratory operation where no final product is discovered, the collection of precursors or listed chemicals is essential in providing evidence of intent to manufacture a controlled substance.

There are many safety precautions that must be taken at a crime scene where controlled substances will be handled. Crime scene investigators should make careful observations and note any conditions which would cause harm to the health of individuals present at the scene. For example, in many clandestine laboratories, it is imperative to ventilate any confined spaces, where there may be poisonous gases present, to prevent inhalation of toxic chemicals by any crime scene investigator.

Evidence Collection and Sampling of Seized Drugs

Prior to 1997, there was no true standardization of procedures or system of checks and balances for the analysis for seized drugs. The Scientific Working Group for the Analysis of Seized Drugs (SWGDRUG) was adopted in 1999, as a result of a consortium between the Drug Enforcement Administration and the Office of National Drug Control Policy (ONDCP), which was formally referred to as the Technical Working Group for Seized Drugs (TWGDRUG). SWGDRUG, which is a committee with international partners, provides best practices and minimum guidelines for the examination of seized drugs. This organization, which is composed of experts in the field of seized drug analysis from around the world, considers international standards when making recommendations for minimum standards for the examination and reporting of seized drugs. SWGDRUG recommendations are submitted to the American Society for Testing and Materials (ASTM), which is an international standards organization that publishes technical standards and best practices for a wide range of industries. Published ASTM standards (2016) in the analysis of seized drugs range from recommended training and educational standards of forensic practitioners to best practices for the analysis of clandestine drug laboratory evidence. Herein, SWGDRUG (2016) minimum recommendations for the sampling and qualitative analysis of seized drugs are discussed.

An important aspect in the collection of suspected controlled substances is determining an appropriate sampling plan. When selecting an appropriate sampling plan, the following questions should be addressed:

- Is the sample population homogeneous?
- Can the net weight of the population be determined from the portion of the population selected?
- What is the confidence level or probability that the chosen portion of the population represents the whole?

The practitioner must choose a sampling strategy, which adheres to the jurisdictional legal requirements and expectations of the customer. For example, if the qualitative analysis or identification of a threshold amount of a controlled substance is sufficient, only a representative sample consisting of portions of the bulk material may be collected and submitted to the laboratory for analysis, while the residual materials may be stored. An additional consideration when sampling is whether either a statistical or non-statistical sampling method will be adopted, which depends on the specific needs of the particular case. For example, in cases where only the presence of any drug in the population is sufficient, a non-statistical sampling method may be appropriate. However, if any inference of the population is to be determined using a portion, a statistical sampling method must be employed. A quick reference guide to drug evidence handling procedures, is provided in Figure 9.1. A more detailed recommended sampling

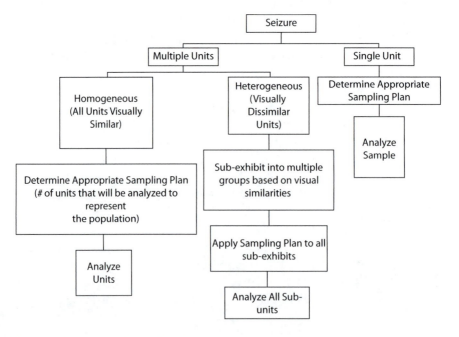

Figure 9.1 Drug evidence handling sampling procedures.

scheme, which can be used to determine an appropriate plan based on the type of seizure encountered, has been recommended by SWGDRUG (2016).

The homogeneity of the evidence sample must also be considered when choosing a sampling plan. If the evidentiary sample is homogeneous, it may be suitable to only collect a single sample. However, if a multi-unit exhibit is encountered, a random sampling, where a number of samples are chosen at random and tested to make an inference about the entire population with a high level of confidence, may be utilized. Standardized procedures for the sampling on materials using statistical methods and probability has been published in ASTM E105 (2016). Ultimately, the most efficient sampling plan, which considers the type of sample encountered, the legal requirements and the reporting expectations and desired outcomes of the particular case, should be used.

Evidence Handling and Collection at Clandestine Laboratories

Clandestine laboratories present a danger to first responders, crime scene personnel, suspects, neighbours or any individuals in a close proximity to the scene. Due to the use of flammable solvents and combustible gas by-products in confined spaces, the risk of an explosion is an added safety concern when processing this type of crime scene. Specific safety precautions must be taken by crime scene practitioners when handling and collecting evidentiary materials at clandestine laboratories, where the manufacturing of suspected illicit drugs takes place. Many of the precursors and by-products, which are encountered by practitioners on the scene of these clandestine operations, are intrinsically dangerous and may expose individuals at the crime scene to numerous chemical hazards and toxic gases. To ensure efficiency and safety of crime scene personnel when a clandestine laboratory is encountered in the field, the following considerations should be addressed:

1. Have proper steps been taken to ventilate the crime scene of poisonous gases or toxic fumes?
2. What synthetic route has been employed?
3. What are the potential safety and chemical hazards, which may be encountered at the scene?
4. What types of personal protective equipment (PPE) should be used to mitigate any possible exposures to hazardous materials?
5. What samples should be collected?
6. How will items be transported and stored for laboratory analysis?
7. How will hazardous waste materials be eliminated safely and within the jurisdictional legal requirements?

Depending on the synthetic route employed, there may be a unique set of chemical hazards and precursors, equipment or intermediate products that must be safely handled and collected. In addition to collecting suspected drug evidence or final product as a result of the manufacturing process, it may also be necessary for the forensic practitioner to recognize intermediate products and precursors, which may be utilized to establish intent to manufacture a controlled substance.

There are a unique set of chemical hazards that may be encountered at a clandestine laboratory by forensic practitioners. It is essential that the forensic practitioner has received specialized clandestine laboratory training associated with different manufacturing methods, possible safety hazards associated with specific manufacturing methods and appropriate evidence handling and collection methods.

A list of possible chemical hazards that may be present at a clandestine laboratory are provided in Table 9.1.

Appropriate PPE should be chosen to mitigate the safety hazards associated with the clandestine laboratory to crime scene personnel. Depending on the manufacturing process used and the type of chemical hazards present, the forensic chemist should determine the type and amount of PPE that should be employed. For example, if poisonous gases and an oxygen-deficient atmosphere is encountered for a specific synthetic route, full air purifying respirator (APR), self-containing breathing apparatus (SCBA) and gas detection devices should be used. As a general rule of thumb, it is always better

Table 9.1   Chemical Hazards at Clandestine Laboratories

Types of Hazards	Specific Hazards
Strong acids/bases	Hydriodic acid
	Hydrochloric acid
	Sodium hydroxide
	Ammonia
Poisonous gases/fumes	Phosphine
	Chlorine
	Hydrogen sulfide
Carcinogenic and mutagenic materials	Mercuric chloride
	Chloroform
	Potassium cyanide
Reactive and air sensitive materials	Red phosphorus
	White phosphorus
	Lithium
Analytical testing incompatibilities	Phosphorus with Raman
	Color tests reagents with cyanide salts (exothermic reactions)
Flammable solvents	Diethyl ether, acetone, methylated spirits
Radioactive materials	Thorium

to initially have an excess of PPE and reduce the amount used after carefully assessing the chemical hazards and determining that particular chemical threats or hazards have been eliminated.

In addition to considering the safety hazards associated with a clandestine laboratory, it is also important to determine which samples should be collected. This may be a challenge for the forensic chemist, due to the variety of precursor and solvent materials used, the intentional camouflaging of chemicals in unapproved containers and equipment or tubing that may contain desired final product or evidence of the manufacturing process. Specialized knowledge and training of synthetic routes, precursor chemicals and products will assist the forensic chemist in determining which samples should be collected as evidentiary items. In general, finished product, intermediates, precursors, key reagents and reaction mixtures should all be collected as evidence. However, in many cases, other materials, such as waste, unlabelled materials and equipment, should also be collected to assist in determining the synthetic route employed. Other considerations include how potentially hazardous materials will be either properly disposed or packaged and stored for further analysis in the lab. The forensic chemist should also be aware of the legal requirements for the safe removal of hazardous waste products. In most jurisdictions, efforts to dispose of hazardous waste products and chemicals are often coordinated with a hazardous materials (HAZMAT) team to meet Occupational Safety and Health Administration (OSHA) standards.

References

ASTM E105-16. (2016). Standard practice for probability sampling of materials. *Annual Book of ASTM Standards*. West Conshohocken, PA: ASTM International.

Schedules of Controlled Substances. Code of Federal Regulations (21 CFR § 812). (2015). *Food and Drugs – Drug Enforcement Administration*, Department of Justice. Washington, DC: U.S. Government Printing Office. available online at https://www.gpo.gov/fdsys/pkg/USCODE-2015-title21/html/USCODE-2015-title21-chap13-subchapI-partB-sec812.htm.

Scientific Working Group for the Analysis of Seized Drugs (SWGDRUG). (2016). *Recommendations*. Edition 7.1. available online at http://www.swgdrug.org/approved .htm.

Evidence Collection and Management for Forensic Toxicology Analysis

10

ASHRAF MOZAYANI

Contents

Traditional Toxicology Samples

Analysis of blood is one of the most widely used interpretative specimens of toxicology analysis. It is particularly useful for the interpretation of drug levels and their metabolites in postmortem and human performance forensic toxicology. For example, blood can be used to determine whether an individual was under the influence of alcohol or other drugs while operating a motor vehicle. A blood analysis can also provide valuable information in postmortem cases, such as the effect of a drug at the time of death or in cases of suspected drug overdose and poisoning (Table 10.1).

Living Subjects

Blood samples should be collected from living subjects as soon as possible. Blood is collected using a syringe and a vacuum tube, usually from the median cubital vein of the arm. Care should be taken to use only nonalcoholic antiseptic wipes for cleaning the collection site on the subject's arm. Two tubes of blood samples should be taken in grey top tubes that contain sodium fluoride and/or potassium oxalate; 10–20 mL is recommended. To prevent loss of volatile drugs such as alcohols, the tubes should be tied closed. Zittel et.al (2006) has shown there is no statistical difference in concentration of alcohol using expired tube up to 74 months beyond the expiration date. A study by Shan et al. (2015) indicates long-term stability of alcohol

Table 10.1   Pros and Cons of Most Common Toxicology Analytical Samples

Specimen	Advantages	Disadvantages
Blood (antemortem)	Best for interpretation of drug and alcohol levels	Inconvenient/intrusive collection
	Correlation of test results to drug effects	Alcohol testing takes longer than breath
	In delayed death investigation	
Blood (postmortem)	Best for interpretation of drug and alcohol levels	Specimen value is dependent on manner of collection
	Correlation of test results to drug effects	Susceptible to postmortem redistribution
Urine	Ease of postmortem collection	Test results do not correlate to drug effects
	Great for drug screening, especially recent use	Ease of adulteration, substitution and dilution
	Sufficient volume for testing	Antemortem collection is easier than blood, but still considered an invasion of privacy and donors may have difficulty providing a specimen
Breath	Non-invasive	Indirect testing for blood alcohol level
	Fast results	Requires cooperation from the patient and cannot be saved for further independent retesting
	Backbone of DUI testing	
Vitreous fluid	Resistant to putrefaction	Limited specimen amount
	Great for postmortem alcohol analysis	Interpretive value of drug analysis may be limited
Liver	Potentially high drug concentrations	Requires sample pretreatment
	Interpretive value	
Gastric contents	Helpful in overdose or poisoning cases	Collection of the entire specimen is needed for interpretation
Brain	Can be useful for narcotics and antidepressant drugs	Drug concentrations can vary depending on the area tested
Bile	Good alternative specimen when postmortem urine is not available	Susceptible to interferences

(*Continued*)

Table 10.1 (*Continued*)   Pros and Cons of Most Common Toxicology Analytical Samples

Specimen	Advantages	Disadvantages
Cerebrospinal fluid	Resistant to contamination	Invasive collection
	Can be useful for drug screening	
Lung	Good specimen for volatile substances like carbon monoxide and cases of suspected huffing	Sample pretreatment is required
Kidney	Good specimen for heavy metal poisonings	Sample pretreatment is required
Hair	Provides up to 90-day drug use history	Possible environmental contamination (particularly from smoked drugs)
	Convenient collection	Drug concentrations can be affected by hair colour and cosmetic treatments
	Non-invasive	Not a sensitive matrix for marihuana testing
	Good for testing of chronic exposure to heavy metals	
	Second sample available for reanalysis	
Nails	Can provide a long window of exposure	Interpretation of results can be difficult
Sweat	Adulteration is difficult	Possibility of environmental contamination
	Less invasive than blood or urine	Relative new technology
Oral fluid	Tamper-resistant method of drug screening	Costs more than urine drug testing
	Ease of collection	Some collection devices provide poor recovery due to absorption of the drugs
	Good indicator of recent drug use	Small sample size
Meconium	Ease of collection	Small sample size
	Long window of exposure	Lack of homogeneity
		Requires low limits of detection

after long-term, unrefrigerated blood stored in room temperature in whole blood. In these cases, negative alcohol blood stays negative. The study also reported that the stability of ethanol after long-term, unrefrigerated storage of whole blood samples. Hence, there is no production of alcohol in preserved antemortem blood samples during long-term storage at room temperature regardless of blood volume or whether or not the sample tube was previously opened. However, concentration in positive blood alcohol samples decreases in room temperature storage and the decrease in concentration is greater if the tube was previously opened or less than half-full. The authors concluded that loss of blood alcohol is independent of the original concentration and can be between 0.01 and 0.05 g/dL for 89% of the cases.

Postmortem Collection

Prompt recovery of postmortem blood is crucial due to postmortem redistribution (PMR), which is well known among toxicologists. Prompt recovery of postmortem blood specimens is important because the quality of samples decreases with time. At least two different sources of blood specimens should be collected from the cardiac and peripheral region. Cardiac blood is more plentiful but is more suitable for qualitative analysis due in part to possible increasing drug concentration from other areas of the body or PMR. Femoral blood taken by direct vascular access is preferable for determining the amount of any drugs present and should be collected whenever it is possible. Approximately 20 mL of cardiac blood and 20 mL of peripheral blood are recommended and these should be collected into grey top tubes that contain sodium fluoride and/or potassium oxalate, unless fluoride poisoning is suspected. To improve interpretation, the quantitation of dugs must be from peripheral blood such as femoral or iliac venous. Ethanol concentrations can also decrease as a result of microbial consumption and chemical oxidation to acetaldehyde. In postmortem, the concentration of ethanol can also increase for the conversion of glucose to ethanol.

After collection, the tube should immediately be stored in the refrigerator during testing and then frozen for long-term storage. Different sources of blood must not be combined.

Urine is the most used specimen for drug monitoring in criminal justice cases involving workplace drug testing. In addition, it is the specimen of choice in drug-facilitated sexual assaults (DFSA) and postmortem drug screens. Most drugs and specifically metabolites are present in higher concentrations in urine and it is a relatively easy sample to analyse. At least 15–30 mL should be collected for living subjects, and all that is available collected from postmortem cases. Specimen preservatives are not required; however, refrigeration is highly recommended. It is important to remember that the presence of a drug in the urine indicates only exposure to the drug and is not indicative of human behaviour.

Vitreous fluid, also called vitreous humour, is a clear gel-like fluid contained in the eyes that is composed mostly of water. Vitreous fluid can be ideal for postmortem analysis because the specimen is uniquely isolated and protected from other body fluids and decomposition is often delayed as compared to other body fluids. In fact, it is the only useful specimen for testing glucose and electrolytes after death. There are several drugs that are more stable in this matrix, such as 6-monoacetyl morphine, and it is a common specimen for alcohol analysis. Vitreous fluid from deceased individuals is obtained by inserting a needle directly into the globe of the eye and drawn 1–3 mL from each eye. All that is available should be collected without a preservative for alcohol and drug analysis.

In cases of suspected poisoning or drug overdose, the analysis of gastric contents can provide valuable information. Sometimes, even the smell of gastric contents is useful; cyanide, ethanol and pesticides each have characteristic odours. All gastric content that is available should be collected; preservatives are not recommended. If there are any visible capsules or tablets these should be removed and stored in a separate container.

Most drugs are metabolized through the liver, making this type of tissue very useful for postmortem analysis. It can be especially helpful for interpretation of blood results for drugs with large volumes of distribution or long half-life that can have exaggerated concentrations due to accumulation in the tissue. The sample should be taken from deep in the right lobe if possible, to avoid potential contamination from gastric contents. As with most other tissues such as brain, kidney heart, a collection of around 50 g into a sealed plastic container is recommended.

Nontraditional Samples

Hair analysis is considered by many to be the best tool for investigating drug-related histories, because drugs can be detected for many months. Collection of the specimen is simplified because there is no need for same-sex collectors and it is non-invasive. Additionally, adulteration of the test is not a likely concern. A bundle of hair that is approximately the size of a pencil should be collected from the crown of the head, cutting the hair as close to the scalp as possible. The end closest to the scalp should be tied and clearly marked. Hair specimens should be stored at normal room temperature.

Oral fluid, or saliva, is a type of specimen that has been gaining a lot of interest in recent years. Oral fluid is sometimes preferred for drug testing because the sample can be collected in the presence of a monitor, or under direct supervision. This makes it difficult for samples to be adulterated or substituted and eliminates potential invasions of privacy. Another advantage to oral fluid is that drugs can usually be detected immediately after use, whereas drugs take more time to become detectable in urine and hair. Detection of drugs in oral fluid is an indication of recent use. Oral fluid could become the specimen of choice for DUI drug screening because of the ease of collection and promising availability of roadside screening. Numerous collection devices are available that involve expectoration, saturation onto a swab or aspiration. Sample sizes are often 1 mL, but the volume collected varies according to the device.

Fetus, newborn and breastfed children can be tested via meconium, amniotic fluid and breast milk. Meconium is the first faecal material of a newborn infant. Toxicology analysis of this type of specimen can be used to determine maternal substance abuse. Meconium is unique because it can provide a more accurate history of drug exposure, particularly within the last 20 weeks. It is best to collect the specimen within 24 hours or less of birth. All of the available sample should be collected and submitted for analysis.

Amniotic fluid fills the amniotic sac inside the uterus. Drugs cross the placental barriers from maternal to fetal circulation by diffusion. The transfer of drug to amniotic fluid tends to increase in late pregnancy due to increased placental blood flow and surface area. The fetus swallows and inhales amniotic fluid and releases urine into it. This allows the fluid to be sampled and tested to evaluate fetal health. A 25 mL sample of amniotic fluid is collected using a procedure called amniocentesis that involves inserting a thin needle through the belly and uterus into the amniotic sac. No preservative is needed.

Breast milk is a combination of water, lactose, fat and protein. It is an easy sample to be tested for monitoring the therapeutic drugs and drug of abuse including alcohol. Approximately 10 mL in a sealed sterile container should be collected via manual expression or breast pump. The sample should be kept in the refrigerator.

Specimen Selection: Type of Analysis

Forensic analytical toxicology is based on screening and mass spectrometry confirmation for all drug testing; however, choice of diverse specimen and detection cut-off are vital for various types of testing such as human-performance drug testing, postmortem drug testing, DFSA drug testing and even pain management drug testing.

The human performance drug testing is the type of testing that seeks to determine the role of alcohol and/or drugs in affecting human behaviour. Breath alcohol analysis makes up the bulk of testing for alcohol-impaired driving. Blood and urine have been choice specimens for a long time, but oral fluid may become more prevalent in the future due to the ease of collection and good indication of recent use.

Drug-Facilitated Crime

Although the public commonly associated gamma-hydroxybutyrate (GHB) and rohypnol with the DFSA, but any other drugs that incapacitate or intoxicate an individual should be suspected and tested such as alcohol. Urine is usually the specimen of choice. Some drugs are eliminated quickly from the body, so it is important to collect and refrigerate a urine specimen as soon as possible. If a suspected crime occurred within 24 hours, a blood specimen should be collected as well. If an assault is reported long after it occurred, hair analysis may provide useful information.

Workplace Drug Testing

Urine is the most common specimen used in workplace drug testing, but oral fluid and hair are viable options. Oral fluid and hair are less susceptible to adulteration and substitution, and collection is less intrusive. One of the advantages of hair testing is that drugs remain present for much longer periods of time (up to 3 months).

Postmortem Toxicology

Decomposition and PMR are two issues associated with postmortem toxicology, and each of these can greatly affect the toxicology analysis. Recommended specimens depend on the type of death, but blood, urine and vitreous fluid are commonly collected. All specimens should be collected and submitted for analysis as quickly as possible. Provide a list of any known medications, or those found at the scene.

Pain Management Drug Testing

Oral fluid and urine are the specimens of choice for monitoring various prescription, non-prescription and illegal drugs.

Specimen Labelling and Packaging

Specimens should be labelled with the following:

- Specimen type.
- Name of individual or other identifier.
- Date and time of collection.
- Collector's information including signature or initials.
- Case number according to agency's criteria.
- Specimen source. For example, in postmortem cases cardiac or peripheral source. If peripheral, from which site venous femoral, iliac, etc. should be indicated.

Safety

It is worthy mentioning that 'universal precautions' during the collection, packaging and any handling of toxicology evidence are crucial. All specimens should be considered as potentially infectious materials. The use of appropriate personal protective equipment, such as gloves, protective eyewear and, in some situations, masks, is recommended. Hands should always be washed after glove removal. Do not eat or drink in areas where biological evidence is handled. Likewise, the storage of food and beverages should be designated and maintained separately from evidence storage. Training in the safe handling of biological specimens is recommended, as well as hepatitis B vaccination.

Conclusion

The interpretation of analytical data in forensic toxicology is not standardized. This results in confusion among those who are responsible for adjudicating toxicology-related cases. Standards for the type of sample collected, the handling of toxicology evidence, storage, a comprehensive drug screen and standardized interpretation of results would assist the triers of fact in determining interpretation of toxicology cases. Cases involving drug testing require a thorough characterization of properly collected evidence and an informed interpretation of results. The critical steps are (1) the collection and preservation of evidence, (2) the submission of the evidence to an adequately equipped laboratory and (3) the interpretation of the findings of these analyses.

The analytical capabilities of laboratories vary widely. Toxicology evidence must be analysed for a large number of drugs, many of which require special techniques and expertise not available in some laboratories. Laboratories that mainly provide clinical laboratory services or occupational urine drug screens are seldom appropriate for forensic toxicology. The lab selected to perform toxicology testing should be able to furnish a report either excluding or confirming the presence of alcohol, opiates, benzodiazepines, tricyclic antidepressants, antihistamines, muscle relaxants, barbiturates, cannabinoids and any other category of drugs.

References

Shan, X., Tiscione, N. B., Alford, I., Yeatman, D. T., and Vacha, R. E. (2015). A study of blood alcohol stability in forensic antemortem blood samples. *Journal of Analytical Toxicology*, 39(6), 419–425.

Zittel, D. B., and Hardin, G. G. (2006). Comparison of blood ethanol concentrations in samples simultaneously collected into expired and unexpired venipuncture tubes. *Journal of Analytical Toxicology*, 30(5), 317–318.

Bibliography

Concheiro, M., Shakleya D. M., and Huestis M. A. (2011). Simultaneous analysis of buprenorphine, methadone, cocaine, opiates and nicotine metabolites in sweat by liquid chromatography tandem mass spectrometry. *Analytical and Bioanalytical Chemistry*, 400(1), 69–78.

The International Association of Forensic Toxicologists. (1999). *Recommendations on Sample Collection (TIAFT-Bulletin, XXIX(1))*. Retrieved from www.tiaft.org.

Karch, S. B. (2007). *Postmortem Toxicology of Abused Drugs* (1st ed.). Boca Raton, FL: CRC Press.

LeBeau, M. A., and Mozayani, A. (2001). *Drug-Facilitated Sexual Assault: A Forensic Handbook*. San Diego, CA: Academic Press.

McLemore, J., Schwilke, E. W., Shanks, K., and Klein, D. (December 2013). *The Effects of Acquisition of Blood Specimens on Drug Levels and the Effects of Transportation Conditions on Degradation of Drugs (NCJRS Document No. 244232)*. Washington, DC: U.S. Department of Justice.

Negrusz, A., and Cooper, G. A. (2013). *Clarke's Analytical Forensic Toxicology* (2nd ed.). London: Pharmaceutical Press.

Samyn, N., De Boeck, G., and Verstraete A. G. (2002). The use of oral fluid and sweat wipes for the detection of drugs of abuse in drivers. *Journal of Forensic Sciences*, 47(6), 1380–1387.

Society of Forensic Toxicologists and American Academy of Forensic Science. (2006). *Forensic Laboratory Guidelines*. Retrieved from http://www.soft-tox.org/files/Guidelines_2006_Final.pdf. September 1, 2016.

United Nations Office on Drugs and Crime. (2014). *Guidelines for Testing Drugs Under International Control in Hair, Sweat and Oral Fluid*. New York, NY: United Nations.

Questioned Documents

11

CLAIRE WILLIAMSON

Contents

The application of allied sciences and analytical techniques to solve questions concerning documents is termed forensic document examination. Documents under examination are referred to as questioned documents and can involve the analysis and comparison of questioned handwriting, typewriting, printing, papers, inks, photocopied documents and other documentary evidence. These documents can be in many different forms including letters, envelopes, currency, cheques, passports, contracts and wills. In many cases, the questioned document is compared with materials of a known origin in an attempt to establish its authenticity or to detect any alterations.

Science is increasingly used in court and is an important part of the criminal justice system. In one year alone, over 150,000 cases were dealt with in the United Kingdom by forensic science providers, covering all areas of forensic science (Parliamentary Office of Science and Technology, 2005). This has created a growing need for more diverse ways to obtain and analyse such materials. It is therefore of the utmost importance that all scientific evidence is obtained in accordance with strict protocols and that any subsequent analyses are appropriate and accurate, so that the integrity of the evidence cannot be put into question. Careful consideration of types of analyses that are carried out is important due to the potential that one analytical protocol may have to interfere with any subsequent tests. If possible, the best procedure to carry out is one that is non-destructive to the sample. This then allows re-examination or further analyses of the evidence, such as DNA profiling or fingerprint examination.

This chapter covers the collection and preservation of items associated with document analysis. It provides general information regarding selection and collection, covering various types of documents as well as more specific information, such as specimen samples for handwriting, counterfeit documents and damaged documents.

Selection of Evidence

At a scene, any item could be potential evidence. It is up to the crime scene investigators and attending officers to determine which evidence should be collected. Knowledge of what potential intelligence can be obtained from the items assists the investigators in making these decisions. Handwriting and signatures are primarily used to determine authorship, but documents can also indicate the source and location of where they were produced, e.g. which office printer was used. Information from the production of the document can also give an indication of when the document was produced; for example, if the chemicals used in the paper even existed at the time it was purported to have been made.

Documents can also be a source for different types of evidence such as fingerprints, DNA and footwear. It is important to prioritize the evidence so that all types of examinations can be completed, in order to assist in the investigation, while not to the detriment of others. It is preferred that all document examinations are completed prior to fingerprint examinations, as many of the techniques used to enhance fingerprints include chemicals which can affect the results of ink analysis (Baxter, 2015).

Questioned Document Collection and Packaging

As with all types of evidence, care must be taken so that no additional damage is caused to the items, resulting in loss of evidential value. They need to be handled with care and, where applicable, should be collected using the smallest area possible, such as handling only one corner. They need to be packaged so that they remain intact and in the state in which they were found. In particular to document examination, no unwanted indentations or marks should be added on to the evidence, especially when packaging and labelling these items. Indentations can be detected through examination but additional indentations can impede investigations, so they must not be produced. If there are multiple sheets of paper, they should not be stapled together.

Gloves should always be worn when handling any documents in question. All items should be packaged individually, unless they are obviously part of the same document. The ideal packaging would be the use of envelopes or paper bags. This will help to keep the documents flat and prevent the addition of any folds, as these can disrupt detail on ink lines (Hilton, 1940). Plastic bags can impede some examinations, such as the use of an

Electrostatic Detection Apparatus (ESDA) to detect indentations (Allen, 2016). The packaging should then be securely sealed and signed. All items collected will be labelled; however, labelling conventions will differ depending on the specific procedures of each organization. While some use physical labels that get attached to each item's packaging, others will have packaging with pre-printed labels that need to be filled in. Either way, it is recommended that the labels are completed prior to the item going into the packaging. When possible, all original documents should be submitted for examination. Photocopies are acceptable, but can limit the examination due to lack of detail present in the photocopy compared to the original, e.g. striations from ballpoint pens, which can identify the pen, but also show the direction of strokes for the letter construction.

In order for a questioned document to be examined, it has to be compared to other samples such as controls. These comparison samples or specimens are extremely important if an opinion on authenticity or authorship is to be made.

Handwriting Comparison Specimens

There are two types of specimen: request and non-request. Request samples are taken directly from the suspect, through which they are asked to produce samples of handwriting, usually with a ballpoint pen. The phrase required can be dictated to the suspect to ensure the appropriate letters and words are obtained for examination. When written, it is advisable that each specimen is removed or obscured from the suspect's view so they are unable to refer back to it when writing the next sample. The suspect should also sign and date each specimen.

The style of writing must be the same as the questioned document, e.g. cursive and cursive, block capitals and block capitals. Cursive cannot be compared to block capitals. For a single line of questioned writing or signature, a minimum of 10 samples would be required, but for a larger document such as a letter, one written sample would contain enough writing for comparison.

Non-request samples are those obtained from the suspect's everyday life, e.g. diary, letter, notebook and shopping list. These samples are extremely useful, as they will contain the natural variation of the writer who produced them. They can also be of use if a suspect has attempted to disguise their writing or has been uncooperative with supplying request samples, as these specimens will not be affected. However, with non-request samples it must be confirmed that they are in fact from the suspected author. The difficulty with this type of specimen is getting samples that contain the correct letters and words needed to compare with the questioned document. It is also important that the time frame in which these samples were produced is equivalent to the questioned document. Multiple factors can affect handwriting such as alcohol, medication, illness and age, so the samples need to be contemporary to the time that the questioned document is believed to have been written.

Typewritten and Printed Document Specimens

Documents that are printed or produced using a typewriter will normally be compared in attempts to determine if the samples were made by the same machine or to establish the source of the specimen's production. When possible the machines themselves should be collected as well as any accessories, for example, the used ribbons from a typewriter. When it is not possible to collect the physical machine, specimens need to be gathered from it and submitted instead. Be sure to take note of the make, model and serial number. As for typewriters, it is important to also replace the ribbon with carbon paper and type out the full keyboard at least three times, as well as the full questioned document, following its exact layout.

For photocopied documents, blank samples are needed. These are obtained with no paper on the platen, with the lid down. A minimum of six copies should be made like so. In addition to those copies, six more samples are then required with a blank piece of paper on the glass platen. Ensure that the size of the samples is the same as the questioned document, e.g. A4, A5 etc.

Counterfeit Documents

If a location is suspected of producing counterfeit documents, it is necessary to seize as much evidence as possible. Types of items that would prove useful for an investigation include any genuine documents that may have been copied, any artwork or photographic images, printing plates and printing material such as test runs. Items that have been discarded can also be useful. For the examination, genuine samples of the counterfeited documents would be required for comparison purposes. Any paper and ink may be used for examination, but if mass produced would be of less evidential value.

Damaged Documents

Documents can be damaged in numerous ways, for example, shredding, cutting and burning, all of which make them extremely fragile. No attempt should be made to reassemble any paper fragments or shifting of fragments from waste containers, as this can hinder the document examination. All content from the container should be recovered and if necessary the container itself. When collecting burnt or charred items, rigid, flat boxes that can be lined with cotton to immobilize the items are preferred.

When collecting wet documents, cardboard sheets can be used to move them onto clean paper towels for drying and packaging. If the documents are folded, they should not be opened. This should only be done by a document examiner. When dry, the items can be positioned between sheets of paper before placing them into packaging. The paper towels used for drying should be retained as they may contain trace evidence from those items.

By following the guidelines above, this will enable a full examination of the evidence to be carried out by the document examiner. They will be able to do handwriting and signature comparisons, indented writing assessments and ink analysis, to name a few.

References

Allen, M. (2016). *Foundations of Forensic Document Analysis.* Chichester: John Wiley & Sons.

Baxter, J. (2015). Questioned document evidence. In *Complete Crime Scene Investigation Handbook* (pp. 419–424). Boca Raton, FL: CRC Press.

Hilton, O. (1940). The care and preservation of documents in criminal investigations. *Journal of Criminal Law and Criminology,* 31, 103–110.

Parliamentary Office of Science and Technology. (2005). Science in Court. Postnote, Number 248.

Forensic Digital Evidence

12

ZENO GERADTS

Contents

Short History

The first cases of digital evidence date from the 1970s and involved the use of computers (Whitcomb, 2002). These cases were mainly focused on financial fraud. In the 1980s, forensic accountants realized that information extracted from computers was the only evidence available. The first commission on digital evidence, the High Technology Crime Investigation Association (HTCIA), was established in 1984 in California. The Federal Bureau of Investigation (FBI) established the Computer Analysis and Response Team (CART) that same year (Pollitt, 2003). Next, several groups developed standards for digital evidence beginning with the Scientific Working Group on Digital Evidence (SWGDE) in the 1990s. The European Network of Forensic Science Institute (ENFSI) (Geradts, 2011; Welch et al., 2012) initiated their own working group in forensic Internet technology in 1997. Many new working groups in digital evidence popped up, and in association with the American Academy of Forensic Science (AAFS) began discussions in 2002 (Jamieson and Moenssens, 2009; Siegel et al., 2013) to establish a new section called the Digital and Multimedia Sciences. In the meantime, several best practice guides including the International Organization for Standardization (ISO) guidelines were published and now software for analysis of digital evidence is part of the mainstream. Forensic science laboratories are often accredited by the American Society of Crime Lab Directors (ASCLD) (Houck, 2013) or their accreditation is based on ISO 17020 or 17025.

Types of Evidence

In digital forensic science, the question that often arises is 'Can this evidence be linked to an individual suspect? (Cohen, 2010). This link is hard to establish at times especially since multiple users can operate an individual computer. Therefore, attribution to a single person is not always possible and individuation of a suspect falls short.

The main tasks associated with forensic digital evidence are given below (Compton and Hamilton, 2011; Saleh et al., 2009).

1. *Data collection* is defined as the correct copying and preservation of digital data. Knowledge of digital storage media such as solid-state disks (SSDs) and hard drives is important to forensic investigation. Moreover, the digital forensic expert must know how to locate the evidence. Further, data collection requires the expert to safeguard the evidence as well as preserve the integrity of the evidence sans any alterations without permission of the requester. In this field, the forensic specialist must be aware of the types of questions that can come up in criminal proceedings. This includes whether or not the bypassing of the access codes has been correctly carried out or if the electronic equipment was properly secured.

2. *Data examination* comprises the investigation of copies made of the digital data sources collected. Digital forensic specialists should be aware of the contextual effects in conducting casework. Within this framework, different files and fragments can be discovered and the appropriate experiments conducted to verify the results. Some of the questions that should be answered in this phase include:
   a. Was the data accessible to the suspect?
   b. Where is the data on the exhibit and by what means has it been retrieved?
   c. Can these methods be validated?

3. *Data analysis* involves the interpretation, reconstruction and analysis of the evidence found in the digital data sources. Several hypotheses have to be tested before the expert can give a qualitative opinion on the evidence. For example, how much knowledge and skill are necessary to take a particular action? Within reconstruction, how did the discovered digital traces end up on the material that was examined? Concerning interpretation, have alternative hypotheses been answered?

For analysis of the digital evidence, many proprietary, open source software and hardware are available. The expert should have knowledge on the reproducibility of the results utilizing different tools. Additionally, forensic specialists should be able to draw a distinction between results given by different tools. Further, versions of different digital products might result in disparate findings.

Ontology

We use the ontology as used by Nickson et al. (Pollitt, 2010; Karie and Venter, 2014) that divides the field into the following categories:

- Computer forensics
- Software forensics
- Database forensics
- Multimedia forensics
- Device forensics
- Network forensics

Computer Forensics

Within digital forensics, server, laptop and desktop analysis can lead to potential evidence. This evidence can be extracted from disk storage or RAM memory from which logs and user data files can be extracted.

Software Forensics

Within the field of computer forensics, the operating system (OS) is an important component for examination. Most often, Windows or Mac (Djukic and Mohapatra 2009; Arimura, 2010; Willis 2014) is utilized. However, in some cases, the open source OSs of Linux and Unix need analysis. Moreover, some devices contain varying OSs from those mentioned. Application software forensics is a wide field where a plethora of apps for different computer OSs as well as the OSs of mobile devices and tablets are constantly updated. Some apps are more widely used than others, creating a better body of knowledge on how to uncover any data collected from them. However, the large number of apps developed each year is so vast that it is impossible to be knowledge-able on data collection and evaluation for all apps. Many of these most pop-ular apps are constantly being updated by the programmers who develop them, thus delivering new versions on a regular basis. Within this specific field of app development, forensic tool analysis is important. Tools like Encase, FTK, Nuix, X-Ways and Sleuthkit were widely used in 2016. Source code analysis is also included within this field, where attribution to authors can be ascertained.

Database Forensics

In database forensics, the importance of database analysis cannot be under-stated. Databases for investigation include bank records, store and other cus-tomer receipts, medical information and the like. A clear understanding of the Database Management System (DMS) utilized is critical in database forensics.

Multimedia Forensics

The field of multimedia forensics is expanding and now includes image, video and audio forensics. Within this field, image source comparison, image forgery detection and authenticity of images are all part of the investigatory process of multimedia forensics. In addition, digital video forensics includes the carving of video when part of the file has been wiped as well as the clon-ing and duplicating of frames. Within digital audio forensics, discovering the time of recording is facilitated by Electric Network Frequency (Elmesalawy and Eissa, 2014).

Device Forensics

Device forensics includes a wide range of instruments. They range from small-scale devices such as smartphones, tablets and GPS tools to large-scale devices in industrial settings. Included in this category are peripheral devices that incorporate printers, copiers and scanners. Additionally, car electronics such as GPS and computer consoles as well as medical devices such as pacemakers are contained within this category. Regularly, memory chips are removed from these devices and read by a proper forensic tool. These tools include Cellebrite UFED, Systeen Secure View and Micro Systemation XRY Baggili et al., 2013).

Network Forensics

Network forensics uses scientifically proven techniques to achieve its goal. In doing so, investigators aim to find evidence related to the planned intent or measured success of unauthorized activities upon a system used to disrupt, corrupt and/or compromise system components. Most often, network forensics deals with dynamic and volatile information. The forensic specialist should watch out for an attacker who can erase all log files. Within this field, other divisions incorporate cloud, telecom network, Internet and wireless forensics.

Packaging of Digital Evidence

Any actions related to the identification, collection, packaging, transportation and storage of digital evidence should be documented. According to Maloney et al. (2014) of the National Forensic Science Technology Center,* when packing digital evidence for transportation the first responder should:

- Ensure that all digital evidence collected is properly documented, labelled, marked, photographed, video recorded or sketched, and inventoried before it is packaged. All connections and connected devices should be labelled for easy reconfiguration of the system later.
- Remember that digital evidence may also contain latent, trace or biological evidence and take the appropriate steps to preserve it. In most cases, digital evidence imaging should be done before latent, trace or biological evidence processes are conducted on the evidence.
- Pack all digital evidence in antistatic packaging.
- Ensure that all digital evidence is packaged in a manner that will prevent it from being bent, scratched or otherwise deformed.
- Label all containers used to package and store digital evidence clearly and properly.
- Leave cellular, mobile or smartphone(s) in the power state (on or off) in which they were found.
- Package mobile or smartphone(s) in signal-blocking material such as Faraday isolation bags and radio frequency-shielding material when the power state is an issue.
- Collect all power supplies and adapters for every electronic device seized.

Transportation Procedures

When transporting digital evidence, the first responder should:

- Keep digital evidence away from magnetic fields such as those produced by radio transmitters, speaker magnets and magnetic mount

* http://www.nfstc.org/bja-programs/crime-scene-investigation-guide/

emergency lights. Other potential hazards that the first responder should be aware of include seat heaters and any device or material that can produce static electricity.

- Avoid keeping digital evidence in a vehicle for prolonged periods of time. Heat, cold and humidity can damage or destroy digital evidence.
- Ensure that computers and electronic devices are packaged and secured during transportation to prevent damage from shock and vibration.
- Document the transportation of the digital evidence and maintain the chain of custody on all evidence transported.

Storage Procedures

When storing digital evidence, the first responder should:

- Ensure that the digital evidence is inventoried in accordance with the agency's policies.
- Ensure that the digital evidence is stored in a secure, climate-controlled environment or a location that is not subject to extreme temperature or humidity.
- Ensure that the digital evidence is not exposed to magnetic fields, moisture, dust, vibration or any other elements that may damage or destroy it.
- Further, during transport and storage the power issue should be taken care of, preferably by utilizing a Faraday cage for storage.

Challenges

Within digital forensic sciences, there are a number of challenges that should be considered (Garfinkel, 2012). Other issues include the use of strong encryption, the heterogeneity of data and the volatility of the evidence. Moreover, the problem with growing amounts of data combined with data storage and backup are issues to overcome.

Several anti-forensics tools have been developed to delete the remnants of data after normal deletion so that data recovery is extremely difficult if not impossible. Along with the short lifespan of software versions as well as the fast developments of new products, the interpretation of all data becomes difficult. For cloud computing, juridical and ethical issues as well as privacy laws pertaining to medical records per se exist and may become problematic.

Furthermore, there are no good standards for making a forensic copy from a cloud service, and the discussion of digital traces and time stamps can be confusing. Issues with locating employee files as well as licensing requirements make evidence collection a challenge. Other issues exist with live systems, such as banking systems, that make it not economically feasible to turn them off and do the forensic investigation.

Quality Assurance

For digital evidence, there are several ISO standards such as ISO/IEC 27037:2012 that provide guidelines for specific activities in the handling of digital evidence. These recommendations are especially important to the first responders on scene and the exchange of digital evidence between different jurisdictions. The ISO standard ISO/IEC 27041 offers guidance on the assurance aspects of digital forensics. For example, these principles ensure that the appropriate methods and tools are used properly. These standards cover both the analysis and interpretation of evidence.

ISO/IEC 27042:2015 provides the guidelines for the analysis and interpretation of digital evidence. Also included in this standard is the evidential control, or the maintenance of the chain of custody and handling of the documentation. The process of interpretation by different investigators should result in similar results, and differences between the results should be explainable in court. This is still a challenge, since different tools might give different results. Proficiency tests and testing competency of the investigator are important in this guideline. The standard ISO/IEC 27043 covers the broader incident investigation activities within which forensics usually occurs. Finally, ISO/IEC 27050 concerns electronic discovery.

Further, many labs are accredited according to ISO 17025 or 17020 and ASCLD standards. The SWGDE-guidelines, ANSI Standards and ENFSI Forensic IT working group best practice guide might help to implement these standards.

Presentation in Court

In court, the presentation of digital evidence might become complex soon, especially in cybercrime cases where anti-forensics software has been used. The judges, jury and prosecutor should have some basic technical knowledge. Depending on the case (e.g. cybercrime cases can be complex if several jurisdictions are involved), the report should be understandable and influences of bias should be reported as well as differences of opinion between experts, if any.

Big Data/Intelligent Search Deep Learning

With the growing amounts of data, methods such as deep learning might also be used in the investigational process (SAS, 2015). For example, based on other case data, one might train a deep learning network with examples of pictures with a concept. These methods should be used in combination with a human and currently a human expert has to verify the results. The validation of the results is important and there is currently no standardization yet on using them in court.

Future Expectations

It is expected that in the next 4 years, forensic data scientists will have more standards that will make results more comparable. Additionally, it is expected that strong encryption causes (Ambadiyil et al., 2015) more live forensic systems to have to be examined. Issues with privacy and ethics in forensic investigations also need resolution. The fast development of apps and their rising numbers make it impossible to interpret all the data in a given case. Triage is necessary to make the forensic investigation more cost effective. Finally, proprietary data formats and incorrectly implemented open formats that are ever changing make it complicated to handle.

References

Ambadiyil, S., Jayan, K. G., Prabhu, R., and Pillai, V. P. M. 2015. Microstructure encryption and decryption techniques in optical variable and invariable devices in printed documents for security and forensic applications. In Baldini, F., Homala, J., and Lieberman, R. A. (Eds.) *Proceedings of the SPIE Optical Sensors 2015 Conference*, 9506, 13–16 April 2016, Prague, Czech Republic. Bellingham, WA: SPIE.

Arimura, H. (December 2010). Software development of an image processing program for Mac. *Nihon Hōshasen Gijutsu Gakkai zasshi*, 66, 1648–1654.

Baggili, I., BaAbdallah, A., Al-Safi, D., and Marrington, A. (2013). Research trends in digital forensic science: An empirical analysis of published research. *International Conference on Digital Forensics and Cyber Crime*, 114, 144–157.

Casey, E. (2011). *Digital Evidence and Computer Crime: Forensic Science, Computers, and the Internet*. Cambridge, MA: Academic Press.

Cohen, F. B. (2010). Attribution of messages to sources in digital forensics cases. In *43rd Hawaii International Conference on System Sciences*, Honolulu, Hawaii, pp. 1–10.

Compton, D., and Hamilton, J., Jr. (2011). An examination of the techniques and implications of the crowd-sourced collection of forensic data. In *IEEE 3rd International Conference on Privacy, Security, Risk and Trust and Social Computing*, Boston, MA, pp. 892–895.

Djukic, P., and Mohapatra, P. (2009). Soft-TDMAC: A software TDMA-based MAC over commodity 802.11 hardware. In *IEEE INFOCOM 2009 – The 28th Conference on Computer Communications*, Rio de Janeiro, Brazil, pp. 1836–1844.

Elmesalawy, M., and Eissa, M. (2014). New forensic ENF reference database for media recording authentication based on harmony search technique using GIS and wide area frequency measurements. *IEEE Transactions on Information Forensics and Security*, 9, 633–644.

Garfinkel, S. (August 2012). Lessons learned writing digital forensics tools and managing a 30 TB digital evidence corpus. *Digital Investigation*, 9, S80–S89.

Garfinkel, S., Farrell, P., Roussev, V., and Dinolt, G. (September 2009). Bringing science to digital forensics with standardized forensic corpora. *Digital Investigation*, 6, S2–S11.

Geradts, Z. (November 2011). ENFSI forensic IT working group. *Digital Investigation*, 8, 94–95.

Houck, M. M. (2013). American Society of Crime Laboratory Directors (ASCLD). In *Encyclopedia of Forensic Sciences* (pp. 198–198). Cambridge, MA: Academic Press.

Jamieson, A., and Moenssens, A. (Eds.). (2009). AAFS. In *Wiley Encyclopedia of Forensic Science*. Chichester: John Wiley & Sons.

Karie, N. M., and Venter, H. S. (September 2014). Toward a general ontology for digital forensic disciplines. *Journal of Forensic Sciences*, 59, 1231–1241.

Maloney, M. S., Housman, D., and Gardner, R. M. (2014). Crime scene investigation. In *Crime Scene Investigation Procedural Guide* (pp. 1–2). Boca Raton, FL: CRC Press.

Pollitt, M. (2010). A history of digital forensics. In K.-P. Chow and S. Shenoi, *Advances in Digital Forensics VI* (pp. 3–15). Springer.

Pollitt, M. M. (2003). The very brief history of digital evidence standards. In *Integrity and Internal Control in Information Systems V* (pp. 137–143). New York: Springer US.

Saleh, H., Agaian, S., and Mohamamd, K. (2009). Digital forensics: Electronic evidence collection, examination and analysis by using combine moments in spatial and transform domain. In *IEEE International Conference on Systems, Man and Cybernetics*, San Antonio, TX, pp. 3489–3494.

SAS. (2015). What Is Big Data? Retrieved from http://www.sas.com/en_us/insights/big-data/what-is-big-data.html. Accessed March 23, 2015.

Siegel, J. A., Saukko, P. J., and Houck, M. M. (Eds.) (2013). American Academy of Forensic Sciences (AAFS). In *Encyclopedia of Forensic Sciences* (pp. 196–196), Cambridge, MA: Academic Press.

Welch, L. A., Gill, P., Phillips, C., Ansell, R., Morling, N., Parson, W., Palo, J. U., and Bastisch, I. (December 2012). European Network of Forensic Science Institutes (ENFSI): Evaluation of new commercial STR multiplexes that include the European Standard Set (ESS) of markers. *Forensic Science International: Genetics*, 6, 819–826.

Whitcomb, C. M. (2002). Forensic aspects of digital evidence: Contributions and initiatives by the National Center for Forensic Science. *Proceedings of SPIE 4709, Investigative Image Processing*, 111, 23–32.

Willis, S. (December 2014). Accreditation – Straight belt or life jacket? Presentation to Forensic Science Society Conference November 2013. *Science & Justice: Journal of Forensic Science Society*, 54, 505–507.

Yeh, C.-C., and Xing, M.-H. (July 2016). Key factors influencing digital content industry in Taiwan from the triple helix perspective. *Technology Analysis & Strategic Management*, 28, 691–702.

Evidence Collection for Arson Cases

13

KENNETH WILSON

Contents

Arson is classified as a Part I crime by the Federal Bureau of Investigation (FBI) Uniform Crime Reports. In 2014, arson was responsible for $729 million in property damage, a 10% increase from 2013. There were 19,000 intentionally set structure fires. Up to 157 civilians were killed as the result of arson fires, up 4.7% from 2013. A total of 42,934 arson cases were reported. Of all major crimes, arson has the lowest clearance rates.

In order to discuss evidence collection at an arson scene, we first must explain the intricacies of arson investigation. In this chapter, we identify several aspects of arson investigation, including what an arson investigator can and cannot do, long-standing myths about burn patterns, what is a competent ignition source, hurdles that have to be overcome in arson cases, what tools are available to the arson investigator and what types of evidence should be collected by the arson investigator.

Who is an arson investigator? Most people believe that the term 'arson investigator' refers only to those who investigate fires that have already been determined to have criminal intent. In fact, the arson investigator and the fire investigator will conduct the very same investigation from the beginning. The only difference between an arson investigator and a fire investigator is, typically, that the arson investigator is a law enforcement official and has the authorities, as such, granted by the state.

Here is the best description of an arson investigator that I have read:

> Part detective, scientist, engineer, and law enforcer, the fire investigator represents the collusion of multiple careers rolled into one. It is the fire investigator who must explore, determine, and document the origin and cause of the fire, establish what human actions were responsible for it, then bring authoritative testimony to the courtroom to win a conviction in cases of arson.
>
> . . . [According to Paul Horgan, accelerant detection canine handler and state trooper assigned to the Office of the Massachusetts State Fire Marshal] You have to be conscientious and have a mind that likes to figure things out. You really can't take shortcuts. You must take your own photographs, collect the evidence, do follow up investigations. In instances of incendiary fires, you must find the criminal'.
>
> . . . This technical aspect of the job requires knowledge of building construction and materials and the effects of fire upon those materials. Evidence preservation methods, the effects of fire suppression, fire behavior and burn patterns are also important technical aspects. Search techniques must also be learned so that fire cause evidence and ignition sources are preserved during the investigation.

> **– Author Unknown**

Unlike many other law enforcement agencies around the country, arson investigators typically do not have the luxury of calling a crime scene technician to a scene to process evidence of the arson. Arson investigation is an extremely hands-on, dirty, labour intensive job. While most people look at a fire scene as total destruction, the arson investigator sees the scene as a puzzle that will need to be built piece by piece. It is the responsibility of every investigator to enter the scene without any preconceived ideas about the cause of the fire. Most arson cases start off as a blank canvas. The investigator does not know if the scene is incendiary, accidental or natural. While hundreds of thousands of accidental fires occur every year, the investigator should be cautioned that each scene must be conducted as if it is a crime until proven otherwise. Upon arrival to scenes, an investigator will typically get a briefing from the incident commander and then conduct a safety walk-through of the scene prior to talking to any witnesses. Keep in mind that as a fire or arson investigator, entry onto a person's property must be conducted in accordance with the applicable laws. If a fire scene is still active and there is a possibility that evidence may be destroyed, the investigator may have the right of entry using exigent circumstances. If the fire has been fully extinguished and a delay has occurred prior to the arrival of the investigator, consent to search or a search warrant (criminal, administrative) should be obtained prior to entry. In some jurisdictions, the adopted fire code provides a measure of support for obtaining the administrative search warrant as these codes require all fires to be investigated. Having secured the right of entry, the arson investigator must enter the scene with an open mind and evaluate the evidence that is present. Fire can be classified as having four different causes. The four classifications are found in the National Fire Protection Association (NFPA) document 921, *The Guide for Fire and Explosion Investigations,* as well as other accepted treatises. It is this document that provides the technical guidance to arson investigators to allow a thorough investigation to be completed. Fires are classified under the following causes: accidental, natural, undetermined and incendiary.

- *Accidental*: Fires in which the cause does not involve an intentional act. These fires include ones that started due to inattention and other circumstances that did not occur intentionally. An example of an accidental fire is a curling iron that was left unattended and was knocked into a plastic trash can by a pet.
- *Natural*: Fires in which the cause does not involve a human act (act of God) including wind, lightning, floods and earthquakes.
- *Undetermined*: Fire in which the cause cannot be proven to an acceptable degree of certainty. This includes fires that have not been investigated or may have been investigated and are waiting for additional data to make a final determination. Some arson investigators will shy away from using an undetermined cause, thinking that they 'have to call every fire'. I often caution new investigators that they need to understand an undetermined cause does not mean that they did not do the job assigned. It simply means that they need to collect more data in order to make a proper determination. Undetermined causes can be prosecuted at a later time if additional data is obtained.
- *Incendiary*: A deliberately set fire, with the intent to cause a fire in an area that it should not be, or cause a fire to spread to an area that it should not be. Investigators should collect all the data available prior to making a determination of an incendiary fire and proceeding with criminal prosecution.

The job of the arson investigator is to conduct a scene investigation utilizing an approved method. The most widely used and accepted method is the 'scientific method'. The scientific method consists of the following:

- *Recognize the need (what is the problem)*: In this instance, a fire occurred and needs to be investigated.
- *Define the problem*: Determine the origin and cause of the fire. The problem in a fire case is that the origin (location the fire started) and the cause need to be determined. Keep in mind that this should be backed by an articulable hypothesis.
- *Collect data*: Facts about the incident, interviews with witnesses, firefighters, property owners and occupants, property information

(appraisals, mortgage and insurance). Additional information may include video surveillance, cellular telephone tower data, etc.

- *Analyse the data*: Based on knowledge, experience and training. Having data is not beneficial, if the data is not analysed. Consult experts in the specific areas to review the information collected.
- *Develop a hypothesis*: How did the fire start? Determine the potential ignition sources and fuel packages, then how the two came together to cause a fire.
- *Test the hypothesis*: Not valid unless the hypothesis can withstand the test. This testing may be conducted or referenced. The Bureau of Alcohol, Tobacco, Firearms and Explosives (ATF), the National Institute of Standards and Technology (NIST) and others have published thousands of tests that are available to investigators.
- Select the final hypothesis.

Using a systematic approach to the evaluating the scene, investigators will typically start from the exterior of the scene and work inward from the least amount of damage to the greatest amount of damage. By conducting an examination of the various burn patterns and levels of damage, the investigator will develop an idea of where the fire started, referred to as the 'area of origin'. The scene must be properly documented. This documentation will include photographs of the entire scene. These should be taken in the same manner as any crime scene photo. The photos should include a wide area photo, followed by a mid-range photo and a close-up of any evidence. Taking photos at a fire scene is difficult due to the nature of the scene. Bracketing of photos will help capture minute patterns visible to the surfaces. Another helpful technique is the use of oblique lighting. Photos of a fire scene are the best method to portray the patterns used in the determination of the origin and cause of a fire. As an investigator, it is important to note that a photo log should accompany any report. While conducting the investigation, any witness photos or videos should be collected and added to the case file. These photos will often show the progression of the fire in the early stages, prior to the arrival of first responders. During witness interviews, have the witness show the location that they observed the fire from and obtain photos of the scene from that location. This will provide a perspective of what the witness was able to see. A crime scene diagram should also be generated. These diagrams can be valuable in the prosecution of the case and will help describe to a jury the location that items were found and orient the scene. Several different types of diagrams can be completed, including a basic floor plan, detailed floor plan, evidence location, char depth and fire movement diagrams. By using a computer-aided diagramming program, the investigator can generate multiple diagrams using layering devices. These diagrams will make the court presentations easier for the jury to understand. Once an 'area of origin' is established, then the investigator must begin to methodically remove debris in layers. Each layer of debris needs to be thoroughly evaluated using scientific methods to determine any evidentiary value. In some cases, the debris will hide or contain evidence of the crime. In such cases, the debris will be collected and analysed further using additional techniques discussed later in the chapter. Keep in mind, as debris is removed, photographs should be taken to document the alterations. This is an area of potential challenge at later court proceedings.

One of the greatest challenges faced by the arson investigator is the inherent fact that the fire itself will destroy evidence. The arsonist is counting on the fire destroying all the evidence of the crime; however, this is more often not the case. Evidence can be found if the investigator takes the time to conduct a thorough examination of the debris. Other factors should also be accounted for in examining the fire scene. A fire will double in size every minute that it burns without successful fire suppression. Upon arrival of the firefighters, additional damage is done to the scene and to the evidence. The firefighters have a job to do and in most cases, they are not thinking about evidence while doing that job. The use of hose streams and certain types of chemical agents will adversely affect the investigation and evidence collection process. Investigators often call the firefighters the 'evidence eradication crew' because of the damage that is caused in successfully extinguishing the fire. Upon arrival to the scene, the arson investigator should immediately begin to document the scene and interview the fire department commanders and initial arriving firefighters to determine what they saw, how they entered the scene, what equipment was used, where the fire was and how it reacted to the suppression efforts. These firefighters possess a wealth of information and can be a great asset in the successful prosecution of an arsonist. By conducting these interviews early, the investigator will establish a general location where the fire started and identify any obstacles that might interfere with the investigation. A more detailed interview of personnel can be conducted at a later time. The use of preprinted questionnaires is helpful in guiding the investigator questions.

Myths about Burn Patterns

In the not so distant past, arson investigators were trained by mentors who passed on the knowledge that the mentors had obtained through the years. Many of these older investigators had received training from another mentor and so on. This was identified as a problem because information that was being passed on was considered believable and never challenged. Today, society demands information that is supported by facts and scientific data. Investigators have learned that some of the burn patterns that were used in the past to convict arsonists were not scientifically sound. A couple of burn patterns that were heavily relied upon as 'solid evidence of arson' include spalling of concrete, annealing of springs, crazed glass, copper beading and char patterns. For most fires, the investigator should be able to identify these patterns and explain the meaning behind them.

Spalling

Spalling is a condition where the concrete, brick and mortar are heated and cause a breakdown in the tensile strength of the material. Spalling can occur as the result of moisture trapped in the material being heated and converting to steam or other materials expanding at different rates. As we learned in junior high school science classes, water vapour will expand approximately 1,700 times in volume when converted to steam. Spalling can occur when the moisture trapped in the concrete is converted to steam and expands. This causes layers of concrete to break in strange patterns that will often resemble a pour pattern and was long thought to be from an ignitable liquid. Through testing, investigators have learned that ignitable liquids poured onto concrete do not heat the surface and create spalling. The laboratory tests prove that the introduction of ignitable liquids actually cools the concrete surface as the liquid creates flammable vapour.

Annealing of Springs

As you examine a mattress or any other type of spring that has been through the intense heat of a fire, you will note that the spring appears to have collapsed. This was long thought by investigators to have been caused by the introduction of an ignitable liquid to the furniture, creating a higher temperature fire than the normal burning of furniture would. As this has been studied in laboratories, we have learned that these springs will anneal (collapse) when exposed to the extreme temperature associated with a fire that has no ignitable liquids added. This has become so commonplace, due to the use of synthetic materials in the manufacture of furniture, that the only value to the investigation is that the temperature can be determined to be higher than the failure temperature of the spring assisting the investigator in determining the direction, duration and intensity of the fire.

Crazed Glass

Crazing is the cracking of glass in small pieces. It is often present at a fire and was long thought to be the result of the rapid heating of glass from an accelerated fire. Through testing, investigators are now trained to understand the cause of glass crazing. As the fire burns and heats the glass, firefighters begin to apply colder water to extinguish the fire. As the cold water contacts the class and rapidly cools it, the glass will crack and crazing will occur. What this does tell the investigator is that the glass was intact at the time the fire-fighters arrived on scene to extinguish the fire.

Beading of Copper Wire

Beading often occurs on copper conductors that are heated above 1984°F. For many years, investigators were taught that the beading of copper wiring indicated that the power was on when the fire started or that the fire origi-nated in the location of the beading. Through the use of laboratory testing, we have now learned that the beading of copper occurs when the fire melts the wiring due to exposure. At the same time, aluminium wiring will melt in small pieces and become fragile. The aluminium wiring will often break and cannot be used as a determining factor in the cause of the fire.

Char

Charring and blistering were long considered reliable indicators of an arson fire. Investigators of old would theorize that the size of the blisters and depth of char could indicate the presence of an accelerated fire. Large blisters were said to indicate an accelerated fire. At the same time, it was taught that the shiny appearance was also an indicator of an accelerant being added. The fact is that charring is the result of the material shrinking during a heating event. This shrinking is caused by the compounds of the material being released in the form of smoke. Charred materials will be found in almost all structure fires. During the fire, wood materials will be heated until a chemical decom-position begins to occur known as pyrolysis. The heating will begin to cause the wood material to 'off gas' water vapour and other materials in the form of smoke. The remaining material is primarily carbon and will resemble blisters or alligatoring. The depth of the char is not a reliable indicator of burn time or intensity, but may be used to help establish the fire spread. There are many variables that affect the char depth including the species of wood, humidity, ventilation effects and any type of finish that is present.

Evidence Collection – Old Methods versus New Methods

In the 'old days', arson investigators would focus the entire evidence collec-tion process on locating ignitable liquids or accelerants that were used to set the fire. No attempts were made to collect evidence of forced entry, finger-prints, tool marks, hair and fibre samples or DNA evidence. Some investiga-tors today still believe that these forms of evidence cannot be successfully collected from the scene of a fire and quickly dismiss these forms of evidence.

Investigators will arrive and identify the location of suspected accelerant evidence, collect the sample and submit the sample to a laboratory for analysis and if the sample does not contain an accelerant, the case is considered unsolvable, placed in a drawer and forgotten.

Through proper training, expansion of collection techniques and equipment and successful prosecutions, arson investigators around the world have learned that a wealth of evidence can be found and recovered from an arson scene. Evidence that was long thought to be destroyed by the fire has begun to be recovered and used in prosecutions. Investigators are being taught to recover fingerprints from various objects such as glass, gas cans, bricks and rocks. These fingerprints, for years, were considered unusable. With proper techniques and equipment, fingerprints on porous or rough objects are being collected and used to identify potential suspects. They are also being trained to collect other forms of forensic evidence including DNA, hair, fibre and impressions. Recently, an investigator was successful in collecting DNA from and arson scene and using that DNA sample to prosecute the suspect. This was the first time DNA was used in Texas to convict an arsonist.

Tools for Identifying and Collecting Arson Evidence

There are many tools available to the investigator today that were not available 25 years ago. Like all tools, these are only as good as the person operating them. As with all tools, problems can and do occur. Some of the tools that are used include basic shovels and garden trowels, alternate light sources, electronic gas detectors, sifter screens and specially trained accelerant and explosive detection canines. It is important that the tools be properly cleaned and maintained. Sifter screens are used to separate debris and help investigators locate small items in the debris. During the sifting of debris, smaller screens can be used to prevent items from being discarded. Other tools that are available to investigators include the use of x-ray and computed tomography (CT) scans of debris. The images will allow investigators to quickly determine if an item of evidence is located in a melted debris pile. Each of these tools comes with a measure of uncertainty and a failure rate. Recent studies conducted on the various brands of electronic gas detectors (sniffers) shows an error rate of between 45% and 55%. The accelerant detection canine shows the best error rate of less than 30%; however, the investigator must remember that the canine cannot identify the specific material. Therefore any sample collected due to a canine alert will need to be submitted to an approved forensic laboratory for further analysis to determine what the material is and if it has any evidentiary value. Additionally, new synthetic materials are made using various hydrocarbon compounds and the canine may alert to these type items. In these cases, the canine has a positive alert for a hydrocarbon compound; it is just not an accelerant that was introduced to the scene by the arsonist. Investigators should also remember that the canine cannot testify in a trial. A chemist will be needed to testify to the findings and the gas chromatography–mass spectrometry (GCMS) graph.

During the collection of arson evidence, care must be taken to avoid cross-contamination issues. Tools, especially knife blades and gloves, should be changed between each article of evidence collected. Other tools, such as shovels should be cleaned between uses. Once the area of possible evidence has been identified, a proper evidence container, approved by the forensic laboratory that will be used, should be marked in accordance to ASTM standards and placed by the evidence. The evidence is then collected and placed in the container. To avoid later questions, place the gloves and tools used next to the evidence container and photograph the evidence. The container is then sealed and secured. Additional photos may be taken showing the evidence container after it has been properly sealed. A word of caution: do not place used gloves inside the evidence container.

Cross-Contamination Issues

Cross-contamination is a hurdle that every investigator must face when conducting a crime scene examination. Cross-contamination is the introduction of forensic evidence to a scene that was not originally present. In an arson case, cross-contamination is primarily considered an ignitable liquid. Cross-contamination can occur from a number of sources during a fire. Firefighters that have fuel on their boots or gloves, refuelling of gasoline-powered equipment inside the scene and using gasoline-powered equipment inside the scene. Each of these is a possible source of cross-contamination; however, studies have shown that gasoline on a boot is no longer detectable after several steps. Other sources of cross-contamination include a firefighter handling items of evidence and leaving fingerprints, DNA, hair, chemicals or microbes added to firefighting solutions that destroy the hydrocarbons and damage to evidence from firefighting techniques. Each of these creates obstacles that must be addressed and overcome in the prosecution of arson cases.

Many jurisdictions have addressed these problems through additional training of both firefighters and investigators, and policy revisions. These include providing training to the firefighters on the 'role of the firefighter in the investigation'. A video was produced a few years ago by the International Association of Arson Investigators (IAAI) and distributed to fire departments across the country. This video provides a brief outline about what the investigators are looking for when they enter a fire scene and what information is needed from the firefighters. Investigators have addressed the problem of cross-contamination through the use of decontamination techniques.

Many agencies now require that investigators clean boots and equipment with soap and water each time they enter the scene. The use of decontamination techniques should be documented in the report.

Documentation

The proper documentation of a fire or arson scene is critical to the future case. Worksheets can be created to assist the investigator in properly documenting the scene. Rather than attempting to build the information from scratch, it is recommended that investigators contact their state Fire Marshal's Office or a larger fire investigation unit and request copies of paperwork and worksheets that are used in these investigations. The ATF publishes a small booklet that will assist the investigator and provide helpful tips for the entire investigation. It all starts upon receiving the call. The investigator should document what time the call was received, who placed the call and what was told to the investigator. Upon arrival at the scene, the investigator should make a habit of documenting which fire and police units are on scene. This will be of great benefit later in the investigation when you approach the individuals and ask for statements. Also note the weather conditions, including wind direction, speed and humidity. This will aid the investigator in determining if ventilation or spontaneous heating are factors in the ignition and spread of the fire.

Upon the initiation of the investigation, the investigator should document the date and time and if any other personnel are assisting. If others are assisting in the investigation, a log should be generated that indicates the assignment. Sometimes, investigators will be given multiple assignments. By completing the Fire Incident Field Notes worksheet, the investigator will obtain the basic data needed to conduct the investigation.

In a fire that has a victim, it is important to document the victim. In some states, a deceased victim can only be manipulated by personnel from the Medical Examiner's (ME) Office. If that is the case in your jurisdiction, photograph the victim and remain present when the victim is examined by the ME personnel. It will also be important to stay in communication with the ME Office to determine the manner of death. Some investigators will be asked to attend the postmortem autopsy. If the fire victim is not deceased, document the injuries including inside the nose and mouth. In most cases, victims are immediately transported from the scene to a hospital. In these cases, the investigator will need to go to the hospital and conduct and interview of the victim. A Casualty Field Notes worksheet should be completed for documenting fire victims.

While conducting the scene examination, it is important for the investigator to articulate in the report any items that are eliminated as the cause of the fire and why. This will avoid a later challenge of 'negative corpus'. The electrical service of a structure is a key element that will need to be examined and properly documented. A diagram of the electrical distribution panel (breaker box) will need to be conducted. Arc mapping is a tool that allows the investigator to determine the general location that a circuit was initially impinged on by the fire. If properly conducted, the arcing event furthest from the electrical distribution panel will be closest to the fire origin. In understanding that once the circuit is impinged on, the breaker will trip and disconnect the power. A good analogy is a water hose. If you kink a water hose, the water is still available behind the kinked area, but no water is available past the kinked area. In an electrical system, the arcing events will prevent power from travelling down the circuit until the breaker trips. If the investigator is not trained in this area, the use of a forensic engineer should be considered. These engineers can often be found working for large local, state and federal agencies tasked with fire investigation or in the private sector. If your jurisdiction does not have access to an engineer, contact the insurance carrier and request that an engineer examine the service. The insurance companies often employ these engineers to examine fires that have a substantial dollar loss. Most states have an arson immunity law that allows the local investigators to obtain reports and other data collected by the insurance carrier for the purpose of the investigation. This will include all reports generated by experts hired on behalf of the insurance company and any interviews conducted with the insured. These statements can be extremely valuable in the later prosecution of both arson and insurance fraud.

Reports generated for arson investigation are not typical of most crimes investigated. These reports are lengthy and complicated. Numerous areas need to be documented. By following the scientific method and using a systematic approach, the investigator will have greater success in prosecuting arson cases.

Conclusion

Arson has long been viewed as nothing more than a property crime. Dating back to ancient times, fire has been used as a weapon of war and a means to destroy the enemy. The intentional use of fire to destroy property or cause injury and death is the crime of arson. It is important that judges, prosecutors and the public begin to view arson for what it truly, is an extremely violent crime that is indiscriminate in who and what is destroyed once it starts. Fire and arson are responsible for hundreds of deaths each year, and the victim is not always the intended target.

As we have discussed in this chapter, fire and arson investigation are highly scientific endeavours that require properly trained and educated investigators. The many aspects of the investigation that have to brought together to form a conclusion requires experts in the field of fire investigation.

We have identified several areas of the investigation that must be properly documented and follow an approved method to reach a final conclusion before it will be ready for prosecution. We have also discussed myths that have been long used to determine the cause of a fire. With the knowledge of today, it is imperative that fire and arson investigators continue to be educated in the latest scientific data available regarding fire causes.

Arson has the lowest clearance rate of all major crimes. It is important that investigators understand the complexities of these cases and better prepare for the hurdles and challenges faced in a courtroom.

Forensic Art and Imaging
Best Practices for Evidence Handling

14

CATYANA R FALSETTI,
ANTHONY B FALSETTI
AND SANDRA R ENSLOW

Contents

Introduction

Forensic art is an expression used to encompass multiple categories of created or altered imagery traditionally used as a law enforcement or an investigative tool. The most commonly used form of forensic visual aid is referred to as composite illustration, whereby an image is created from a witness description and used to include or exclude individuals in an investigation. The other types of forensically relevant graphical representations discussed in this chapter include forensic facial reconstructions or reproductions, postmortem images enhancements and age progressions. Although there are additional types of artistic creations fashioned by a designated forensic art specialist, including image clarification and courtroom exhibits, we will be focusing primarily on the evidence handling of composite sketches and images created from human remains (the postmortem and facial reconstructions).

Because forensic art includes the creation of images that are used during the course of criminal and civil investigations, which may be used during formal legal proceedings. Thus, they must be considered as items containing potential evidentiary value and must be handled in accordance with accepted policies for maintaining the chain of custody in order to be considered as admissible in court. Negligence of the appropriate processes for preserving the chain of custody could result in meaningful exculpatory evidence being disallowed. The handling of image-based evidence starts when a formal request is made for assistance from inside or outside the artist's agency.

Composite Drawings

Composite drawings are by definition made up of various parts of the face, which are then blended or merged together with the intent that the resultant image bears a likeness to the witness' memory of a suspect. The term composite is used because historically the creation of a portrait was made up of different features a witness had chosen from a reference book, and then the characteristics were assembled to create a unified image. A law enforcement agency may request to have composite images generated to represent an unknown person they are interested in locating. A composite drawing is any portraiture that is created by interviewing a witness to create a likeness of an unidentified suspect. The National Center for Missing and Exploited Children (NCMEC) uses the term composite drawing to refer to their age progressions as they are made of a combination of youthful images of the missing child and that child's parents. Features of the child's parents at a given age then are amalgamated to represent a future age for the missing person.

As a matter of practice, the evidence is the image derived from a witness account and the integrity of the witness' account must be protected, as in the case of all other forensically significant documents.

The Overall Interview

Before interviewing the witness, the artist should avoid showing any images of possible suspects as this may unduly influence the final portraiture that is created by the artist. The artist specialist must go into the interview with an unbiased perspective when interacting with the witness. A forensic artist is solely there to create an image for use in the investigation, and not to interrogate the witness or develop additional information about the event beyond the potential suspect's likeness.

The interview should be conducted in a quiet, undisturbed space. It is best if the forensic artist is not wearing a uniform or any agency-issued clothing, but be dressed professionally, which will help the witness feel relax and confident in the process.

The detective may want to watch the interview, as he/she may gather additional information from the witness. If so, it is recommended that the observer not be in view by the eyewitness, as this may deter the witness during the interview. The investigator may watch through closed circuit video, an attached room, or if absolutely necessary, have that person sit behind the witness, out of direct line of sight and caution them not to speak. This is true for any parent or guardian ad litem that may be required to stay in the interview room.

A face-to-face interview is ideal and allows the artist to assess how engaged, cooperative and sincere the witness is in generating an evidence image. Stress, exhaustion and deception can have bearing on the interview, which is an additional reason that an in-person meeting is ideal, to give the forensic artist the greatest understanding of the interview dynamics.

The optimal interview should be conducted in a quiet room with no other images, including wanted posters or booking photos, to distract the witness' focus. The nature of the investigation does not always allow for this preferred environment; however, it should be the goal of the artist to create an optimal atmosphere. Interviewing in less than ideal conditions does happen due to the dynamics of the investigation.

The Cognitive Interview Process

As a general rule, it is best to employ the cognitive interview process when engaged with a potential witness. This is a form of interview practice designed to elicit the most memory and is distinct from the interrogation type interview. This is especially critical with witnesses having difficulty recalling the event due to lapse of time or trauma, among other stressors. Cognitive-based interviews are designed to enhance the ability of a witness to retrieve a memory without compromising accuracy of factual information and are based on the psychological processes of memory and cognition, social dynamics and communication (Fisher and Geiselman, 1992). Seeking and receiving formal training in the method of cognitive interviewing is vital to the success of the interview and the evidence image generated.

Draw Only in the Witness' Presence

The composite drawing is a collaborative process between the artist and the witness. Once the interview is over, your image drawing is finished. Do not alter the actual facial image once your witness has left, since the drawing is theirs, not yours.

Continuing to draw on the image outside of the witness' presence is an unacceptable procedure. To work on the drawing for hours or days and then have the witness come back to approve it is not an ideal procedure. Issues of credibility and image tampering can be raised during court proceedings and can be avoided by proper documentation of the image. Exposing the case and yourself to these issues can be avoided by staying within acceptable guidelines of the interview process.

Signing the Evidence Document

Signing the artwork is not a matter of artistic pride but an accepted evidentiary procedure. Endorsing on the front or on the back is acceptable. Your last name or initials, agency and date are needed at a minimum. You may also have the witness initial the document to illustrate that the witness approved the illustration. Including the case file number is also encouraged so that the image can be accessioned directly – the agency you work for may have further specific protocols to follow and, if not, should be encouraged to develop best practices.

Interview Sheet

It is highly recommended that an interview sheet, or note page, be used. Often, court cases will take years to be resolved, and the artist may be called to testify at a much later date. Interview sheets should include descriptors about the suspect and document the photos witnesses chose from a facial catalogue book. Documenting the date, time, investigator and agency, case number, witness, a translator, interview location and forensic artist will assist others if this case goes dormant for a decade or two. Make sure you fill out all of the boxes of the interview sheet. If items are left blank, then attorneys may question this omission. If a box is not applicable to the particular case or situation, then mark those items N/A. If the witness does not remember then indicate that as well, as their memory or lack there of will certainly be reflected in the final illustration.

Facial Imaging Catalogue

It is highly recommended for beginning forensic artists to use a facial catalogue book for image reference. Some veteran artists do not use, or rarely employ, a facial catalogue book. Both approaches are acceptable. If you use a catalogue, be sure to fully reference the book that you are using and the images the witness selected on the interview sheet.

Delivery of the Drawing

Delivery of the imagery evidence to the investigator should be timely. Every agency may have specific procedures, but the basic standards are outlined here.

- Document and preserve the drawing, by scanning or photographing, to create a digital image.
- It is advisable to scan the document at a higher resolution, 300 DPI or above, and save that scan. The larger size image may be used for press conference display boards (32″ × 40″).
- Then save a base line of 300 DPI and an image size of 1000 K approximately, in JPEG format to send to requesting parties.
- Keep a digital copy of the scans, as well as paper copies of the image and a copy of the notes generated for your files.
- Email the investigator a lower resolution JPEG for use in wanted posters, websites and for sharing with the media.

Send or deliver the evidence package (drawing and notes) to the investigator. Pack the drawing in an acetate sleeve for protection. The drawing is an evidence product and is part of the case. Agencies have developed different protocols but overall the best procedure is to keep the evidence drawing with the case, not the artist. This is especially true for freelance artists. Advise your investigator that the drawing and notes are generally discoverable.

Drawings are generally done on a 9″ × 12″ page format approximately to be able to fit into a scanner and ultimately a file. Some artists draw on larger paper and need to photograph or use a larger scanner.

Arrangements can be made for these drawings. In some agencies, these oversized drawings are left with the forensic artists to store but are still considered evidence. It is recommended that the artist keep a hard copy and a digital copy in an organized and secure filing system for the unit's records.

Forensic Facial Reconstructions or Approximations

A facial reconstruction is an image of a face that is created using the skull of an unknown decedent along with the relevant reports about the case. This form of artistic rendition is used as a tool to aid in the identification of found unidentified human remains.

Receiving the Skull

The skull is the evidentiary property of a medical examiner's office or coroner, depending on the jurisdiction. Although the request to create a facial reconstruction may come from law enforcement, the chain of custody will be through the custodial office. A chain of custody document signalling the physical transfer must be signed, dated and retained by both offices. An artist may receive a skull in person, or via a mail carrier service. In all situations, a paper trail must be kept and recorded for the final report. Before signing for the skull, open the packaging and inspect the skull. Document what and condition of the items, ideally with a photograph, and the number of pieces (mandible, or if the skull is broken) present. Notate that on the document you sign.

The required reports for the most accurate reconstruction are:

- Anthropologist report to indicate the age, sex and ancestry of the individual
- Pathologist report including any photographs of the decedent when first found as any soft tissue on the body would assist with the accuracy of the reconstruction
- Crime scene photographs of the body and any clothing found at the scene
- Any hair found at the scene, including the length and colour after being washed

The reconstruction may be created using clay, hand sketch or via computerized two-dimensional (2D) or three-dimensional (3D) software by placing the skull in the Frankfort horizontal position for photographs, using the appropriate tissue depth measurement charts and formulae for the size and shape of the nose and mouth. The mandible will have to be attached to the crania; it is recommended that an adhesive that is acetone soluble be used for this purpose as well as the attachment of any tissue depth markers.

After the creation of the reconstruction carefully remove any clay or glue that was used. The bones of the mid-face are particularly fragile so it is important to only handle the skull at the strongest points and to manipulate the fragile aspects of the face as little as possible.

The crania and mandible should be photographed and repackaged again. Document the date and time that it was returned or sent back to the originating office. Note the process, tissue depth charts and formulae used in the creation of the image in your report along with any chain of custody information.

Postmortem Drawings

Postmortem images are created to assist with the identification process when an unknown decedent is found and cannot be identified through other methods. This differs from the facial reconstruction done when a cadaver is found while still in the early stages of decomposition.

The goal is to create an image that will make the decedent look more presentable, and as in life rather than as a cadaver may present. This includes adaptation to remove any evidence of violence or damage to the face as well as opening of the eyes and repositioning of the jaw and adaptation of the width of the face to be more in line with how the person would have presented in life.

The optimal situation is to be able to view the actual cadaver while it is still fresh and either take photographs as needed or direct the method and perspective that the photographs are taken. The decedent's face should be photographed with the mouth closed, and jaw held forward. The photographs should be taken from above the decedent at a 90° angle, as well as laterally from each side at a 90° angle. This should be done after the decedent's face is cleaned in the examining room.

Creating the postmortem image may be performed at the morgue or at your office, depending on the timeliness and other logistical factors.

Often, for older cases, postmortem images can only be done with photographs and case information. It is helpful to have any photographs of the decedent when he/she was found at the scene, the height and weight of the decedent to help the artist understand the body size and shape, as well as any clothing found at the scene. It is also beneficial to have the hair cleaned and measured to have a more accurate understanding of the decedent's hair colour and style.

Delivery of these finalized facial reconstructions and postmortem drawing images are similar to the composite art procedures of delivery.

Summary

Traditionally images and other work products created by a forensic art specialist have not always been considered to have evidentiary value. We recommend that forensic art specialists develop standard operating procedures for their units or themselves and implement them for every type of work product created. This will ensure that the chain of custody is maintained and that consistency and surety exist for each investigation.

Reference

Fisher, R. P., and Geiselman, R. E. (1992). *Memory-Enhancing Techniques for Investigative Interviewing*. Springfield, IL: Charles C Thomas.

Bibliography

NPIA. (2009). *Facial Identification Guidance*. Bedfordshire: National Policing Improvement Agency.

St. Yves, M. (Ed.). (2014). *Investigative Interviewing: Handbook of Best Practices*. Toronto: Thomson Reuters Publishers.

Taylor, K. T. (2000). *Forensic Art and Illustration*. Boca Raton, FL: CRC Press.

Wilkinson, C. (2008). *Forensic Facial Reconstruction*. Cambridge: Cambridge University Press.

Ethical Issues, Bias and Other Challenges to Forensic Evidence Management

15

CAROL HENDERSON,
RYAN SWAFFORD AND
ADAM H ITZKOWITZ

Contents

As with most investigations, criminal forensic investigation begins with the evidence that is identified by forensic practitioners and law enforcement officials. After being labelled, field-tested and categorized, the evidence is transferred to the various forensic and law enforcement agencies that will play a crucial role in the outcome of the investigation. Numerous individuals in the chain of custody will contribute their expertise and knowledge to help understand what the evidence means and how it can be interpreted to meet the needs of the investigation.

In some ways, this process is akin to the game of telephone that children play in grade school, where one student's description of an object is relayed to another, thereby passing it through a chain of fellow students who intercept and relay the information down the line. Most often, the initial description is transformed into something only faintly resembling the first student's words, now composed mostly of bits and pieces of the initial information, as some of the message is jumbled and lost by each student along the way. Similarly, the first inspection of a crime scene and the identified evidence will be passed along the respective chain of custody to be analysed by crime scene technicians, law enforcement officials, laboratory analysts and ultimately the participating lawyers and legal professionals. Each has their own responsibilities and objectives in the criminal investigation, so they will include their interpretations and results as needed in the investigatory process. While many procedural rules and ethical guidelines exist for personnel involved in a criminal investigation, the individuals testing the evidence and formulating conclusions are subject to human cognitive biases and contextual factors that can affect even the most experienced forensic specialists. Unconscious biases can be especially difficult to identify and pragmatically impossible to eliminate. However, specialized training and education in ethical conduct and evidence management can be a potential safeguard for the contaminating effects of human cognitive bias in the forensic investigatory process.

Of course, there is no one-size-fits-all answer on how to minimize human error or contextual influences in forensic sciences. The forensic investigation process is time consuming and cumbersome, making it difficult to determine exactly when, where and how a piece of evidence or scientific analysis becomes contaminated, if at all. Considering the breadth of a criminal investigation and the sensitivity of modern forensic techniques, reducing the potential for contamination will depend heavily on available resources as well as a firm understanding of the origins of forensic evidence contamination.* As best stated in the National Commission on Forensic Science (NCFS) Directive Recommendation for a National Code of Professional Responsibility for Forensic Sciences, 'Most forensic science practitioners are committed, hard-working, ethical professionals; however, education and guidance on professional responsibility is uneven and there is no enforceable universal code of professional responsibility' (National Commission on Forensic Science [NCFS], 2016a). Efforts to promote professional responsibility among forensic practitioners and quality management of forensic laboratories have been promoted most recently by Attorney General Loretta Lynch on September 6, 2016 (NCFS, 2016b; Lynch, 2016).

A fundamental challenge to any ethical code is the impracticability of universal adherence by all participants' subject to the code, especially where financial and personnel resources are scarce.† Continuous adherence to a professional code requires education and experience-based training for individual forensic practitioners within all forensic disciplines. First-hand experience and practical training on the ethical dilemmas that each forensic specialist may encounter in the field can help strengthen universal adherence to the code. It mitigates the effects of human cognitive and contextual bias that pose a threat to a forensic investigation (Dror and Charlton, 2006). Standardized ethical guidance and training could potentially reduce contamination by extraneous influences and thereby increase the likelihood that a particular forensic scientist remains objective throughout their analysis (Venville, 2010).

---

* Balk (2015); see also National Commission on Forensic Science (2016b).
† National Commission on Forensic Science (2016a) supra; See also Emily (2016); Bien (2016).

The following hypothetical example will illuminate some of the instances in which appropriate ethical guidelines can proactively strengthen the quality of forensic evidence by reducing sources of bias as well as the effects of human cognitive errors:

The date was Saturday, July 23, 2016. It began like any other Saturday afternoon in the middle of a humid Florida summer. Teens and young adults were enjoying the day off, making their rounds through the local coffee shops and neighbourhood stores, getting as much out of the weekend as possible. It all appeared normal for the City of Gulfport, where individuals in a hurry to get home were juxtaposed with those in a hurry to forget that Monday's responsibilities were approaching. However, this Saturday afternoon wasn't going to be just any afternoon, not with the new Pokemon Go game sweeping across the globe the week prior. This Saturday was different. It was a race to 'catch them all' (Pokemons that is) before the plethora of other players in your orbit caught them first. This afternoon was to be a hunt for many young adults and teens competing with their friends to determine the best virtual Pokemon player, or worse to realize just how much time they were willing to dedicate to catching virtual made-up animals conceived over 10 years ago. Unbeknownst to the thousands of players in Gulfport, an infamous hacker and international terrorist was planning a horrific attack using the Pokemon game itself. The hacker realized that people, after being notified by their friends on social media that the Pokemon they desired had appeared, would travel any distance to 'catch' a rare new Pokemon character. The hacker knew this was the easiest covert method of gathering hundreds if not thousands of people into a single location by inserting the rarest and most desired Pokemon character at a predetermined location of his choosing: a location near a densely populated metropolitan area entrenched in the new mobile game craze that had been downloaded 15 million times by July 13th, the fastest of any app in history.

The timing had to be just right, without a single person in the park paying any attention to the influx of so many rare Pokemon characters in this one location. That's when the explosion shook the universe of the hundreds, maybe thousands of individuals who unknowingly walked into the criminal's horrific trap. With the click of a button from his computer, the criminal hacker behind the cyberattack detonated his homemade bomb disguised as a generic water fountain. Without warning, the park was covered in a cloud of smoke and dust while most individuals previously attempting to catch Pokemon characters turned their attention to the location of friends and family in the aftermath of the terrorist attack.

After the rubble settled and the initial shock from the explosion wore off, bystanders began contacting local law enforcement and emergency response units. The first responding officer arrived just minutes after the explosion and attempted to usher individuals to safety while he also secured the crime scene for detectives and crime scene technicians to follow. After the scene was cleared and secured, the crime scene technicians began assisting law enforcement officials in identifying and collecting evidence that was deemed important or necessary for the ongoing investigation. Local news cameras and bystanders were at the scene, spreading word of the investigation almost immediately after the tragedy took place. News reports broadcasted the carnage quickly with the promising hope that the suspect responsible for this tragedy would be caught. After the lead investigator on scene gave news reporters an 'inside scoop' on the investigation and whom they suspected as a culprit, the information spread like wildfire. Coincidentally, the crime scene technicians overheard the detective's statement to the press while presumptive testing and the lifting of fingerprints found on shrapnel from the explosion were being processed. The premature identification of the suspected terrorist as a U.S. citizen and member of the Gulfport community was publicized to virtually every news station in the area.

Just hours after delivering latent prints, shrapnel, cellular devices and other physical evidence to the local crime laboratory, a positive fingerprint identification and suspect name were provided to the lead detectives. The suspect was identified using a partial match found at the scene, with little additional evidence provided through law enforcement and eyewitness testimony. The suspect was identified as a 35-year-old male, a local resident of Gulfport, Florida. Unbeknownst to the detectives, the suspect's identity was also released to a mayoral candidate, who decided to include this sensitive information in his press release the following day. When the Gulfport Police Department arrived at the suspect's home to assess the scene and ask for his cooperation with their investigation, news cameras and interested bystanders stood ready to accuse this man of committing the heinous act, without regard to what little evidence existed at this point in the investigation. Law enforcement officials were now stuck between a rock and a hard place. The only way officers and examiners would remain employed by the city of Gulfport to solve the now infamous case of the 'Pokemon Go Bomber' was to follow through with the criminal prosecution of the only person of interest already in custody. To the public, this suspect planted the bomb even though the forensic evaluation and police investigation were far from complete. Not only was the physical evidence still being processed at the state crime laboratory, but also federal agents spearheading the digital forensic investigation just received notice of the attack when the suspect was already being interrogated by local police.

The only evidence linking the suspect to the crime was a partial fingerprint found on a destroyed piece of metal found at the park, the same park the suspect happened to take his own children to on occasion. It was unclear to law enforcement how the suspect was able to manipulate the Pokemon Go application platform to allow him to control over the location where the creatures randomly appear in the game. The suspect would then have to notify individual users of his chosen location, in order to lure hundreds of people to the same spot simultaneously. Only after a positive identification was made with the fingerprint did the FBI receive the initial incident report and the detailed descriptions of the crime scene upon first arrival. The FBI and local law enforcement were now working together to determine exactly who was behind the bombing and how the suspect gained control of the game without alerting the game's developers or leaving a clue indicating the suspect's identity. Considering that the only evidentiary link to the prematurely identified suspect is a partial fingerprint comparison, the digital forensic investigation may be the only reliable way of ensuring the right person is charged with the crime.

The explosion itself marked the beginning of a long and exhausting forensic investigation, involving various state and federal agencies, officers, and forensic specialists, that together laid the foundation for a criminal prosecution of the person responsible. Marking the initial communication in the semi-analogous game of telephone, law enforcement and forensic technicians must now begin recording and disseminating their findings of the crime scene for testing and analysis. Local law enforcement will need to ensure that all pieces of collected evidence are properly analysed and that the laboratories used can produce accurate results and conclusions. The FBI on the other hand will likely lead the digital forensic investigation to determine how the criminal took control of the game's administrative server without being noticed by the company's digital security system. Data and physical evidence collected must make their way through technicians, laboratory scientists, detectives and other law enforcement personnel before finally making it to the courtroom where it will be used to criminally prosecute the person identified through the investigation. There are countless instances in which ethical issues can arise during a forensic investigation and it will be the responsibility of each individual actor to do everything practicable to ensure the objectivity of the investigation and the reliability of all conclusions produced.

Challenges to Forensic Sciences

While a hypothetical provides a rather straight forward example of how ethical dilemmas and cognitive biases can permeate the investigative process, research performed by individuals from various scientific, academic and professional communities, including Itiel E. Dror, Jennifer L. Mnookin and Max M. Houck, provide detailed accounts of the plethora of issues that are caused by 'erroneous forensic science' (Mnookin et al., 2011). The initial collection of evidence at a crime scene, in addition to every subsequent action, are critical instances in which every participant of a forensic investigation must stand ready to appropriately handle issues and circumstances that can detrimentally impact the quality of the forensic evidence produced. Biases stemming from cognitive and contextual factors have been an important consideration for both administrative committees and individual scientists whose goals are improving forensic science (Venville, 2010; Fraser-Mackenzie et al., 2013). The implementation of procedural guidelines for forensic institutions and practical training for the consumers of forensic evidence could better prepare forensic practitioners to handle a variety of situations that can, and sometimes do, jeopardize the reliability and effectiveness of the criminal justice system (NCFS Directive Recommendations [2015–2016]).* Ethical issues and other challenges can emerge with little warning and present enormous complications in the criminal justice system, especially in cases of intentional 'dry-labbing', such as the one in which a Massachusetts state crime laboratory scientist, Annie Dookhan, was determined to have been involved in nearly 40,000 criminal cases during the time she was tampering or failing to test evidence.†

Ethical challenges can be present in virtually every phase of a forensic investigation. This is especially true during the analysis of physical evidence in crime laboratories, where untrained or unmonitored laboratory analysts can allow human cognitive influences, or sometimes a more nefarious personal influence, to taint a forensic investigation. Bias, in various forms, has proven one of the most formidable opponents to forensic science, already leading to several overturned convictions and the dismissal of criminal charges (Kassina et al., 2013). In addition, chain-of-custody issues and the objectivity of the scientific analysis performed are some of the more common areas of dispute during the criminal investigation and prosecution. It is the duty of legal professionals to authenticate scientific evidence and expert witness testimony. It is generally in the opposing counsel's best interest to extensively test the veracity of the scientific evidence and expert testimony. On the other hand, it is the duty of the forensic scientist or expert witness to ensure that the scientific evidence is properly tested and reliably explained to the trier of fact, which in most cases is a panel of jurors who do not have, nor are they expected to have, knowledge of the scientific methodologies utilized. While many protocols exist for state funded crime laboratories and other forensic service providers, ethical behaviour is often best learned by experience and

---

* National Commission on Forensic Science (2015) (Acknowledging the "heavy reliance" on forensic evidence stemming from the 2009 NAS Report and the inability of the consumers of forensic evidence, including judges and lawyers, to properly assess and apply this information); parenthetical from NCFS or OSAC directives.

† Jacobs (2013); Dror et al. (2013); Mnookin et al. (2011) (This article grew out of a conference held at the UCLA School of Law in February 2010 under the auspices of PULSE); Augenstein (2015).

discipline-specific training for forensic practitioners.* While some reports of tainted forensic evidence are caused by the intentional acts of an individual involved in the forensic investigation, many others have resulted from the lack of pragmatic and experiential training on how to properly handle the ethical issues that can arise in virtually any forensic investigation.[†]

Since the NAS 2009 Report 'Strengthening Forensic Science in the United States: A Path Forward' and the United States Supreme Court case *Daubert v. Merrell Dow Pharmaceuticals, Inc.* (1993) judges and lawyers alike have been pressed to seek additional information about scientific theory and methodology used by expert witnesses, placing the forensic evaluation process itself under a legal microscope.[‡] As a result, the Department of Justice established the NCFS to develop Directive Recommendations (policy recommendations) for the attorney general and views papers for the community in general. NCFS also promotes scientific validity, interdisciplinary communication and improved federal coordination of forensic science service providers (FSSP).[§]

The advancement of technology and the increased emphasis placed on scientific evidence has brought challenges to forensic disciplines such as fingerprints, ballistics, hair samples, shoe impressions and mixed-sample DNA analyses after various federal agencies began reviewing the accuracy of the results.[¶] The 'Daubert Trilogy' (*Daubert v. Merrell Dow Pharmaceuticals Inc.,*[**] *General Electric v. Joiner*[††] and *Kumho Tire Co. v. Carmichael*[‡‡]) imposed a more demanding standard for judges and lawyers to inquire into the validity of scientific principles used by an expert witness. In addition to the validity of the expert's application of those principles, *Daubert* has also

---

* See Bowen (2010).
† Dror et al. (2013); Federal Bureau of Investigation, FBI Testimony on Microscopic Hair Analysis Contained Errors in at Least 90 Percent of Cases in Ongoing Review (April 20, 2015); see also Russell (2009).
‡ National Research Council (2009); see also *Daubert v. Merrell Dow Pharmaceuticals, Inc.*, 509 U.S. 579 (1993); National Commission on Forensic Science (2015).
§ National Commission on Forensic Science (NCFS), Homepage (https://www.justice.gov/ncfs); Organization of Scientific Area Committees for Forensic Science (OSAC), About Page (https://www.nist.gov/topics/forensic-science/about-osac).
¶ National Research Council (2009). See also PCAST (2016); Shelton (2008).
** See *Daubert v. Merrell Dow Pharmaceuticals, Inc.*, 590 U.S. 579 (1993) (the Court held that the judges are the gatekeepers of scientific evidence, and in performing that function, they must evaluate the following factors regarding the principles and methodology in questions: whether the testimony's underlying methodology is scientifically valid and properly applied to the facts at issue; whether the theory or technique in question can be [and has been] tested; whether it has been subject to peer review and publication; whether it has a known or projected error rate; if it has maintained standards controlling its operation; and if it has attracted widespread acceptance within a relevant scientific community.)
†† See *General Electric v. Joiner*, 522 U.S. 136 (1997).
‡‡ See *Daubert v. Merrell Dow Pharmaceuticals, Inc.*, 590 U.S. 579 (1993); *General Electric Co. v. Joiner*, 522 U.S. 136 (1997); *Kumho Tire Co., Ltd. v. Carmichael*, 526 U.S. 137 (1999).

brought challenges to legal professionals and expert witnesses attempting to admit scientific evidence in a clear and verifiable manner.* In cases that rely heavily on technical scientific methodologies, lawyers and judges are expected to investigate and understand scientific methodologies employed by expert witnesses and prepare a thorough examination thereof to assist the jury. Many legal professionals lack the scientific expertise 'to properly assess and apply' forensic evidence as required by current evidentiary standards despite the 'heavy reliance' on such evidence by the criminal justice system (NCFS, 2015). As a result, forensic practitioners and expert witnesses are often in a position of authority on a particular scientific subject, placing the burden of accurately and reliably applying a valid scientific methodology for the court on the expert testifying. The 'dealings, reporting of data and presenting of opinions to attorneys, judges and juries', as well as the availability of information to the legal professional on how to deal with the increasing complexity of scientific expert testimony are only a fraction of the instances in which ethics must be present and identifiable for verification by the courts.†

Widespread inquiry into the veracity of forensic evidence and increasing pressures to maintain expanding certification, accreditation and procedural standards have uncovered a serious need for capacity building, training and applied research in forensic laboratories. In some cases, crime laboratories have been temporarily shut down or restricted for inadequate procedural safeguards or intentional misconduct by laboratory analysts (Executive Office of the President. President's Council of Advisors on Science and Technology [PCAST], 2016). With increased scrutiny of forensic practitioners and crime laboratories, U.S. Attorney General Lynch adopted significant portions of the NCFS's Recommendation to implement and oversee a Code of Professional Responsibility among Forensic Practitioners.‡ In addition, in September 2016, the PCAST released an extensive report on the status of forensic sciences. The report expresses a need for 'clarity about the scientific standards for the validity and reliability of forensic methods' and the 'need to evaluate specific forensic methods to determine whether they have been scientifically established to be valid and reliable' (PCAST, 2016). The movement towards a better equipped legal community and a more uniform code of conduct for forensic practitioners is expected to reinforce the validity of those scientific methods deemed reliable while also identifying those methodologies that are unreliable or not yet accepted by the relevant scientific community.

---

* See supra.
† See Bowen (2010, pp. 61–73).
‡ Memo for Heads of Department [U.S. Attorney General Loretta Lynch – announcement on September 6, 2016 to adopt PR code for forensic practitioners].

Ethics

Another dilemma investigators face is the ethical rules that govern every phase of the investigation. Procedural and ethical rules have been established, formally or de-facto, for many individuals involved in criminal investigations including law enforcement officers, forensic service providers, criminal attorneys, expert witnesses and judges. However, comprehension and enforcement of ethical rules can often be difficult, if not impossible, to quantify in practice. Some state and local forensic institutions may not even have formal rules and the ethical guidelines customarily followed are more of a moral high ground as opposed to a formal rulebook with discrete penalties. In the absence of a formal written policy, industry norms and customary practices have generally informed forensic practitioners and laboratories, but have also been increasingly difficult to reconcile in the courtroom. As Robin Bowen has stated '[t]hough expert witnesses have no formal rules for testifying in court (besides rules of evidence regarding the admissibility of their testimony), there are some common informal rules to follow' (Bowen, 2010, pp. 61–63). These informal rules for experts and forensic scientists alike include not discussing an ongoing case with anyone outside of court or the laboratory, ensuring that there are no relatives or personal friends involved in a case, and verifying that the methodology behind the testimony or scientific conclusion is objective and relevant.* Accrediting organizations such as the American Society of Crime Laboratory Directors/Laboratory Accreditation Board (ASCLD/LAB) and the American National Accreditation Board (ANAB) have implemented a code of ethics for all accredited member laboratories which acts to ensure compliance with ethical rules within the forensic communities.†

As with formal or informal rules, they are at times broken, whether borne out of necessity, insufficient experience or the lack of practical training of the individual practitioner. Some examples of ethical misconduct in forensic science include planting evidence at crime scenes, collecting evidence without a warrant by claiming exigent circumstances and falsifying laboratory examinations.‡ Even if the crime scene technician or the laboratory scientist are never called to testify in a criminal trial, their recorded data and scientific analyses will be used by at some point in time to prepare for trial. It is important to remember that the law has defined an expert's role as

---

* Bowen (2010), supra, pp. 60–64.
† American Society of Crime Laboratory Directors (ASCLD), Code of Ethics (http://www.ascld.org/wp-content/uploads/2014/08/Code-of-Ethics.pdf); American National Accreditation Board (ANAB), Heads Up (http://anab.org/programs/isoiec-17021/heads-up/) (ANSI-ASQ National Accreditation Board).
‡ Bowen (2010, p. 73) ('Unprofessional conduct includes any action that may tarnish the reputation of an agency or enable the public to lose trust').

'an impartial educator who assists the triers-of-fact by providing specialized knowledge to help decide the outcome of a case' (Bowen, 2010, p. 69). In situations where an expert relies entirely on the recorded scientific analysis performed by others, the reliability and objectivity of each forensic specialist in the chain of custody must be verified by the lawyers and ultimately accepted by the judge as trustworthy.

Research from Saul Kassin, Itiel Dror and Jeff Kukucka indicated that all forensic evidence, even in the more sophisticated FBI forensic laboratories, can be contaminated by human cognitive biases and contextual influences of which the individual analyst or witness is not even aware (Kassina et al., 2013). This is true in nearly every stage of a forensic investigation, including the information and opinions to which a crime scene technician is exposed, whether or not the result is intended. From the crime scene to the courtroom, ethical guidelines and practical training for forensic service providers have and will continue to play an important role in shaping the outcome of criminal trials and the evidentiary hearings that have become even more common after *Daubert*.[*]

Bias

Cognitive, contextual and confirmation bias are problems that affect the reliability of conclusions in many fields including forensic science. Cognitive bias refers to ways in which human perceptions and judgments can be shaped by factors other than those relevant to the decision at hand. It includes 'contextual bias', where individuals are influenced by irrelevant background information; 'confirmation bias', where individuals interpret information or look for new evidence, in a way that conforms to their pre-existing beliefs or assumptions; and 'avoidance of cognitive dissonance', where individuals are reluctant to accept new information that is inconsistent with their tentative conclusion. The biomedical science community, for example, goes to great lengths to minimize cognitive bias by employing strict protocols, such as double-blinding in clinical trials.[†]

---

[*] Bowen (2010, p. 107) ('While having a code of ethics indicates the credibility and willingness of organizations to take responsibility, not having a code does not indicate irresponsibility of the profession. Many times the provisions set forth in a code of ethics are incorporated into codes of conduct of an agency or group'.)

[†] Executive Office of the President President's Council of Advisors on Science and Technology (PCAST): Forensic Science in Criminal Courts: Ensuring Scientific Validity of Feature-Comparison Methods, Section 2.4 (September 2016) (https://obamawhitehouse.archives.gov/sites/default/files/microsites/ostp/PCAST/pcast_forensic_science_report_final.pdf).

We want independent, unbiased opinions from experts that ignore extraneous pressures and influences. Several strategies have been proposed for mitigating cognitive bias in forensic laboratories, including managing the flow of information in a crime laboratory to minimize exposure of the forensic analyst to irrelevant contextual information, such as confessions or eyewitness identification, and ensuring that examiners work in a linear fashion, documenting their findings about evidence before performing comparisons with samples from a suspect.

In a study titled 'Contextual Information Renders Experts Vulnerable to Making Erroneous Identifications', Dr. Itiel Dror sought to analyse how contextual bias affected the Madrid bombing investigations, in which one man was accused of a crime when analysts matched his print to one of the unknown fingerprints found at the bombing. Dror began this study by using the analysis report of a fingerprint that was found at the scene of the Madrid train bombing in 2004.* The study included five examiners who were asked to analyse prints from a crime scene, but they were examining prints that each of the examiners individually worked with from a previous case in which they declared the print a match to a suspect (Dror et al., 2006). These examiners were randomly picked, but had to satisfy certain criteria. First, Dr. Dror needed access to these examiners past matches and secondly, these examiners must have had no knowledge of the fingerprint found in the Madrid Bombing.

For the experimental print comparison, a co-worker approached each of the five participating examiners and told them (1) to examine a set of prints, one from a latent print taken at a crime scene and the other a print obtained from a suspect, (2) that the prints were the same prints that were erroneously matched by the FBI as the Madrid bomber, giving an extraneous context that the prints did not match, (3) to decide if there was sufficient information available to determine whether the print was a match or a non-match, and if so, what was the conclusion, and (4) to disregard the context and background information and focus solely on the print in their evaluation.

From the study, three of the five examiners deviated from their prior findings that the prints were a match and instead changed their findings entirely by holding that they did not match. One of the examiners who previously declared a match now held that there was not enough information to know one way or the other. Of the five examiners, only one of them remained consistent in their findings, holding that the print was still a match. This study, which had four of five examiners changing their positions based on the contextual data they were now receiving, proves that fingerprint examiners are subject to 'irrelevant and misleading contextual influences'.†

* National Clearinghouse for Science, Technology & Law, 'It's Evident' webpage (http://www.ncstl.org/news/Lack6-06).
† Dror et al. (2006), supra note 4, at 76.

In a follow-up study, Dror and Dave Charlton, a veteran fingerprint examiner and supervisor of the UK's police department fingerprint lab, presented to six different fingerprint experts a set of eight pairs of prints derived from a crime scene and a suspect from a previous case in which they actually worked on and declared a match. The criteria for this study was that the participants could not know they were taking part in a study, and either no information was given with the set of prints or that the suspect was either in custody or confessed. The results of this study were staggering. The study surmised that contextual information in the custodial condition of the suspect produced a variance of 17% from the previously correct matches (Kassina et al., 2013).

Studies such as these led the U.S. National Academy of Sciences (NAS) to research the fingerprint identification process. In their study, NAS concluded that it was not scientifically plausible to claim a zero-error rate in the process (National Resource Council, 2009). Additionally, some British police offices have made systematic changes to their process, notably by preventing investigating officers from coming onto the crime scene while awaiting results, and forbidding talking to other investigators involved in the case. However, as noted in the NAS report, in Britain, the forensic division is separated from other police forces, as opposed to the United States, in which fingerprint identification is usually done inside the police department (Spinney, 2010). Such a situation has led to a recommendation by NAS that this policy should change, ultimately leading to criticisms from PCAST and other organizations regarding the accuracy of forensic disciplines and the efficacy of the expert witnesses' testimony explaining the methodologies and error rates of the discipline.[*] Examples of disciplines currently being re-evaluated for accuracy include fingerprint analysis and bite-mark evidence, each of which has undergone increased scrutiny after the discovery of inaccuracies and wrongful convictions due to the reliance on unreliable scientific evidence.[†]

All of this begs the question, if there is not a procedure in place to mitigate the risks associated with cognitive bias in fingerprint investigation, and it is not plausible to claim a zero-error rate in that process, how can we expect the courts to admit the evidence of this investigation into the courtroom and allow the trier of fact to weigh it? In fact, Federal Rule of Evidence 702, and many similar state laws, requires not only the expert's methodology to be reliable, but those same principles must have also been applied in that case.

The American justice system is based on full disclosure of all relevant facts, after the judge, acting as gatekeeper, has decided what the jury may

---

[*] PCAST (2016) (In response to the 2009 NRC report, the latent print analysis field has made progress in recognizing the need to perform empirical studies to assess foundational validity and measure reliability.)
[†] PCAST supra.

or may not hear. It is with that principle that the jury may then form their opinion as to the guilt, or lack thereof, of the defendant. However, if the courts will not prevent this evidence from reaching the ears of the jury, is it fair to a defendant on trial that we allow a jury to weigh what they are hearing? Most members of a jury are not well educated in science, perhaps asking them to determine if one has a cognitive bias, thus resulting in a faulty investigation may be asking too much of them. Despite all of this, courts tend to hold that whether an expert has applied a particular methodology goes to the weight of the evidence, and therefore, the jury should be the one to determine its merit. However, if a group of experts, such as those in the Dror study, cannot come to the same conclusion on a particular point, how can we expect a jury of lay people to be able to do the same?

Conclusion

While ethical issues and bias may never be eliminated since human beings continue to play an integral role in forensic science and law, individual practitioners have made great strides in improvement in recent years with the NCFS Directive Recommendations, ethical codes and Forensic Science Error Management Conferences held by NIST (National Institute of Standards and Technology, 2015). This chapter has pointed out some of the most concerning issues facing forensic practitioners, as well as the proposed solutions being developed by the forensic science and legal communities since the release of the 2009 NAS Report. There is still a long way to go on the path to improving forensic science and the product of forensic investigations; however, advancements in the forensic science community, including the PCAST report regarding key directives will significantly improve the reliability of forensic evidence (PCAST, 2016).

References

Augenstein, S., Digital Reporter, and Allocca, S. (Eds.). (May 2015). 40,000 Cases Poised for Review in Massachusetts Drug-Lab Scandal, *Forensic Magazine*. http://www.forensicmag.com/article/2015/05/40000-cases-poised-review-massachusetts-drug-lab-scandal.

Balk, C. (Spring 2015). Reducing contamination in forensic science. *Themis: Research Journal of Justice Studies and Forensic Science*, 3, 223-224.

Bien, C. (June 2016). DNA Samples in Travis County Cases Will Undergo Extra Scrutiny, Kxan. Retrieved from http://kxan.com/2016/06/13/dna-samples-in-travis-county-cases-will-undergo-extra-scrutiny/.

Bowen, R. T. (2010). *Ethics and the Practice of Forensic Science*. Boca Raton, FL: CRC Press.

Dror I. E., and Charlton, D. (2006). Why experts make errors. *Journal of Forensic Identification*, 56, 600.

Dror, I. E., Chalton, D., and Peron, A. E., (2006). Contextual information renders experts vulnerable to making erroneous identifications. *Forensic Science International*, 156, 74.

Dror, I. E., Kassin, S. M., and Kukucka, J. (2013). New application of psychology to law: Improving forensic evidence and expert witness contributions. *Journal of Applied Research in Memory and Cognition*, 2(1), 78–81.

Executive Office of the President. President's Council of Advisors on Science and Technology (PCAST). (September 2016). Forensic Science in Criminal Courts: Ensuring Scientific Validity of Feature-Comparison Methods. Retrieved from https://www.whitehouse.gov/sites/default/files/microsites/ostp/PCAST/pcast_forensic_science_report_final.pdf.

Fraser-Mackenzie, P., Dror, I., and Wertheim, K. (2013). Cognitive and contextual influences in determination of latent fingerprint suitability for identification judgments, Final Technical Report, DOJ/NIJ Grant #2010-DN-BX-K270.

Jacobs, S. (February 3, 2013). Annie Dookhan Pursued Renown Along a Path of Lies, Boston Globe. Retrieved from https://www.bostonglobe.com/metro/2013/02/03/chasing-renown-path-paved-with-lies/Axw3AxwmD33lRwXatSvMCL/story.html.

Kassina, S. M., Drorb, I. E., and Kukuckaa, J. (2013). The forensic confirmation bias: Problems, perspectives, and proposed solutions. *Journal of Applied Research in Memory and Cognition*, 2, 42–52. Retrieved from http://web.williams.edu/Psychology/Faculty/Kassin/files/1%20Kassin%20Dror%20Kukucka%20(2013)%20-%20FCB.pdf.

Lynch, L. E. (September 6, 2016). Recommendations of the National Commission on Forensic Science, Announcement for NCFS Meeting Eleven. Retrieved from https://www.justice.gov/opa/file/891366/download.

Mieure, E. (July 2016). Crime Lab: Some Evidence Isn't Worth Dealing With, Jackson Hole News & Guide. Retrieved from http://www.jhnewsandguide.com/news/cops_courts/crime-lab-some-evidence-isn-t-worth-dealing-with/article_ff689e2e-2d03-5459-816d-5fbbfec48f83.html.

Mnookin, J. L., Cole, S. A., Dror, I. E., Fisher, B. A. J., Houck, M. M., Inman, K., Kaye, D. H., Koehler, J. J., Langenburg, G., Risinger, D. M, Rudin, N., Siegel, J., and Stoney, D. A. (2011) The need for a research culture in the forensic sciences, *UCLA Law Review*, 58, 725.

National Commission on Forensic Science (NCFS). (December 8, 2015). Forensic Science Curriculum Development, Training on Science and Law Subcommittee. Retrieved from https://www.justice.gov/ncfs/file/818206/download.

NCFS. (March 2016a). Recommendation to the Attorney General National Code of Professional Responsibility for Forensic Science and Forensic Medicine Service Providers, Recommendation developed by Interim Solutions Subcommittee. Retrieved from https://www.justice.gov/ncfs/file/839711/download.

NCFS. (March 22, 2016b). Recommendation to the Attorney General National Code of Professional Responsibility for Forensic Science and Forensic Medicine Service Providers, Recommendation developed by Interim Solutions Subcommittee. Retrieved from https://www.justice.gov/ncfs/file/839711/download.

NCFS. National Code of Ethics and Professional Responsibility for the Forensic Sciences, Directive recommendation developed by the Interim Solutions Subcommittee. Retrieved from https://www.justice.gov/ncfs/file/788576/download.

National Institute of Standards and Technology (NIST). (July 20–24, 2015). International Forensic Symposium: Forensic Science Error Management. Retrieved from https://www.nist.gov/news-events/events/2017/07/2017-international-forensic-science-error-management-symposium.

National Research Council. (August 2009). Strengthening Forensic Science in the United States: A Path Forward, Committee on Identifying the Needs of the Forensic Sciences Community. Retrieved from https://www.ncjrs.gov/pdffiles1/nij/grants/228091.pdf.

Russell, S. (2009). Bias and the Big Fingerprint Dust-Up, Pacific Standard. Retrieved from https://psmag.com/bias-and-the-big-fingerprint-dust-up-9c554fa2ac20#.det1xup3m.

Shelton, H. D. E. (March 17, 2008). The CSI Effect: Does It Really Exist?, National Institute of Justice. Retrieved from http://www.nij.gov/journals/259/pages/csi-effect.aspx.

Spinney, L. (March 18, 2010). The Fine Print, Macmillan Publishers Limited, Vol. 464. Retrieved from http://nebula.wsimg.com/695d3d7b0eddffe1b0096a2f41989a24?AccessKeyId=09634646A61C4487DFA0&disposition=0&alloworigin=1.

Venville, N. (2010). A Review of Contextual Bias in Forensic Science and Its Potential Legal Implications, The Victoria Law Foundation Legal Policy Internship Program, Partnered with the Australia New Zealand Police Advisory Authority and the National Institute of Forensic Science (ANZPAA-NIFS).

Index

A

Accidental fires, 153
Adhesive surfaces, 26–28
American justice system, 182
American National Accreditation Board
    (ANAB), 179
American Society for Testing and Materials
    (ASTM), 119
American Society of Crime Laboratory
    Directors (ASCLD), 179
Ammunition, firearms evidence, 113–116
ANAB, *see* American National
    Accreditation Board
Anal examination, 52–53
Anthropological specimens, 62–63, 68–69
Arc mapping, 161
Arson Immunity law, 161
Arson investigation
    computer-aided diagramming program,
        154
    copper wire beading and charred
        materials, 157
    cross-contamination issues, 159–160
    destroying evidence, 155
    documentation, 160–161
    evidence collection, 157–158
    fires, classification of, 153
    scientific method, 153–154
    spalling and annealing of springs, 156
    tools, for identifying and collecting,
        158–159
ASCLD, *see* American Society of Crime
    Laboratory Directors
ASTM, *see* American Society for Testing
    and Materials
ASTM E1188-11 – Standard Practice for
    Collection and Preservation of
    Information and Physical Items,
    94
Autopsy collection, 66–68

B

Batting method, 90–91
Biological evidence
    collection and preservation of, 37–39
    description of, 29–30
    practical considerations for collection
        of, 32, 37
    reference sample collection, 40–41
    scene of crime, 30–32
Burn patterns, 155–156
    beading of copper wire, 157
    crazed glass, 156–157
    spalling and annealing of springs, 156

C

Cardiac blood, 128
Cartridge casings, firearms evidence,
    111–113
Chain of custody, 53
Clothing, 49
Cognitive bias, 173, 175, 180–183
Cognitive interview process, 165
Collection, evidence, 7
Collection sheet, evidence, 12
Colposcope, 50–51
Combing method, 87
Composite drawings, 164–167
Computer forensics, 143
Confirmation bias, 180
Consent, for sexual assault, 47
Contextual bias, 180, 181
Controlled Substances Act, 117
Counterfeit documents, 138
Crime scene
    for detectives and technicians, 173, 174
    diagrams, sketches and scanning
        systems, 5–6
    documentation, 4–5
    evidence collection, 9